The Fascinating World of Helen Bonfils

By Eva Hodges Watt

WESTERN REFLECTIONS PUBLISHING COMPANY®

Lake City, CO

© 2007 Eva Hodges Watt

All rights reserved. No part of this book may be reproduced in any form without permission in writing from the author.

ISBN 978-1-932738-43-8

Library of Congress Control Number: 2007928683

Cover and book design by Laurie Goralka Design

First Edition

Printed in Canada

Western Reflections Publishing Company®
P.O. Box 1149, 951 N. Highway 149
Lake City, CO 81235
1-800-993-4490
westref@montrose.net
www.westernreflectionspub.com

For Rob, Joe and Laura

More than anyone I have ever known, Helen was a different person to everyone who knew her. You would find it difficult to find any two people who saw in her the same person. She carried the theater into real life. But one thing everyone would agree upon was her ability to make every person she met feel that she loved them.

— Donald Seawell, Helen Bonfils' attorney and chief executive officer, *The Denver Post*

INTRODUCTION

Strikingly tall and blond, for three decades she was known as Denver's Lady Bountiful. On specified days the needy lined up at her office door to collect hand-written checks. Her contributions built Holy Ghost Church in downtown Denver. She gave liberally to hospitals and other good causes. She was the angel behind Broadway hits and she even had parts in some of them. She grew up in a fifty-room mansion in Denver, and her sumptuous two-story New York apartment on East River Drive commanded an unsurpassed view.

And in her late sixties, while her dashing cosmopolite husband lay gravely ill, she seduced her chauffeur, a semi-literate hustler one-third her age. Eventually, she married him, spent millions to finance his remarkably successful ventures as an oilfield wildcatter, and tolerated his indiscretions as he pursued the beautiful Las Vegas singer Phyllis McGuire.

She is, of course, Helen Bonfils, younger daughter of Frederick Bonfils, the garish and astonishingly successful newspaper tycoon who claimed relationship to Napoleon Bonaparte.

So incredible is Helen Bonfils' story that it is difficult to separate fact from fiction. What follows, then, are the recollections of friends, associates and confidantes who knew Miss Helen, suffered her whims, shared her secrets, admired and loved and pitied this remarkable woman.

It is not likely that we will see her kind again.

— William Hosokawa

CHAPTER ONE

MISS HELEN AND THE TIGER

Denver was not Helen Bonfils' kind of town. Denver, as she told her friend Haila Stoddard, was "a meat and potatoes town." Her idea of a real city was New York. Still, Denver was home, and as she saw it on a spring day in 1972 from her sixth-floor suite in St. Joseph's Hospital, it was preening greenly at its best.

Denver is a city of trees, and spring had leafed out the big old elms so that a tapestry of tender green spread for miles below her toward the skyline of proliferating skyscrapers. Beyond these, the blue, blue mountains wore shining white caps. She wouldn't see the trees in their autumn gold that fall. But she would not let her thoughts drift in that direction. She had a great deal of time to think, and a realization that may have dawned on her was one that had long distressed her friends: that is, she was damned dumb about men.

Helen believed that Papa—her father, Frederick G. Bonfils—was the greatest man she ever knew. But if there was one thing she might have faulted him on, it was that he did his level best to prevent Helen and her sister May from having any knowledge about the opposite sex. They were sent to girls' schools from first grade through finishing school. They weren't allowed to date, at least not as other girls did. They didn't go to parties and picnics. Not for the

Bonfils girls were the tango dances at the Cosmopolitan Hotel after World War I or the trips to the mountains in the newfangled automobiles. They certainly didn't kick up their heels in the Junior League Follies, which didn't accept Helen until, in her mature years, she was named an honorary member.

So May eloped with the first man she went out with. And she had to sneak out her bedroom window to see him at that. The results were, for her, disastrous. Seeing Papa harden his heart against May, his favorite, was enough to keep Helen single and in line until after he died.

By then Helen was forty-four and she, too, married the first man who had an opportunity to court her. Not that her marriage to George Somnes, the director of Elitch's Theatre, wasn't happy or that they weren't well-suited. Helen adored being an actress, being directed by George, and working with all the talented actors she met at Elitch's, Denver's summer theater. They were mad, witty, irrepressible individuals, the kind of people she had longed for. After their marriage, Helen and George began producing plays in New York. She furnished the money, he directed, and she acted in their productions. What an audacious dream they had! And some of it came true. Well, money can do that. They had an absolutely fabulous two-story apartment overlooking the East River. There wasn't a better address in Manhattan. Helen adored New York.

She worshipped the world of big-time theater, the opening nights followed by champagne buffets in the River House apartment, and someone running out to get the newspapers so they could read the reviews (even if they were often disappointing). She could shop to her heart's content on Fifth Avenue, from Bergdorf's to Bonwit Teller, to the atelier of her favorite designer, Elinor Jenkins; she could attend the theater any night of the week and revel in the city's other myriad charms.

"Magnificent, mysterious New York," E.B. White wrote, and, it would seem, he spoke for Helen. She was truly fond of dear, dowdy old Denver, but in her opinion it would forever be a cowtown.

She often told people that George was the love of her life, and she believed that. He had the wonderful Barrymore profile that reminded her of Papa's. And he was so witty; Spring Byington, an actress of Hollywood fame, a dear friend who acted in the Elitch's company for several seasons, swore he was the wittiest man she ever knew. George had absorbed "culture" growing up in Florence, Italy; he had fought in World War I and traveled the world over. He directed in Hollywood before he came to Elitch's. George was so soignee, so intelligent, so sophisticated. And so disinterested in a physical relationship with Helen (or any woman) that it was a fairly bloodless marriage.

So, enter Mike, their chauffeur. Mike had a very healthy interest in the opposite sex. George employed him in 1950 after Helen developed phlebitis and needed a strong-backed young buck to carry her up and down the stairs and to and from the limousine. Mike wasn't tall and handsome. He was "sort of good-looking, in a gangsterish way," as Helen's friend Gretchen Weber put it. But he had a wiry strength that came from pounding spikes on the railroad in Nebraska, and when he scooped Helen up in his arms and she nestled against that warm, muscular chest— well, little thrills she had never felt before raced through her bosom, as her friend, *Post* columnist Bill Barker, rhapsodized. This, she must have told herself in surprised amazement, is a real man.

George died from liver failure in 1956; it seemed he couldn't really drink New York and Denver dry as he appeared to think he could. Helen's affair with Mike began while her husband lay dying down the hall in the house on Washington Street, according to her servants. Her friend Haila Stoddard believed Helen suffered pangs of guilt about this preemptory intimacy.

Friends and business associates describe meetings with Helen in her boudoir during which she reclined on a chaise lounge wearing, typically, a gorgeous peignoir revealing her voluptuous bosom. One of them, *Post* photographer Dave Mathias, recalls his discomfiture when he called with some photographs she had requested he bring. Helen patted the lounge and said, "Sit down, Dave dear," and proceeded to go through the pictures, sitting thigh to thigh beside him. "I got out of there as soon as I could," Mathias said. "But, later, I would think, 'Hey, I might have ended up owner of *The Post.*'"

So, it is not difficult to imagine that Helen may have extended a similar invitation to her chauffeur, who called on her each morning to discuss her plans for the day. And, in the hours they spent together, riding in the limousine, or at home, it would be in Helen's

Denver Post photographer Dave Mathias was devilishly handsome, so when Helen's glance lit on him, it lingered. Shown here with *Post* reporter and author Eva Hodges in 1953. *Author's collection.*

nature to encourage the young man to expand on his ambitions to become an oil wildcatter. It was a subject he could talk about with passion at length, she discovered. She began backing Mike, investing what would eventually be millions of dollars in oil rigging and other equipment

Mike was much younger than she, of course—twenty-five to Helen's sixty-one years. But her age was something Helen never admitted.

In any event, Helen didn't care. She wanted Mike. When they were apart, she thought about him obsessively, according to Haila. When Helen was with him, she felt so much younger, she said. In New York, they went to the zoo in Central Park and to Jack Dempsey's Restaurant, where darling Jack gave her big bear hugs. Helen and Mike went to the circus at Madison Square Garden, to the theater, and to movies and restaurants. She hadn't laughed so much in years.

It didn't even matter that her eyes were almost level with the top of his prematurely balding head when she was wearing her customary stilt heels. Or that he was a grade-school dropout, smart and sassy and frequently crude and ungrammatical—so unlike the proper people who usually surrounded her.

He was especially different from George, dear urbane George, so suave with his pencil-line moustache, handsomely turned out in his dark, pinstriped suits and homburg. George, so coolly unemotional.

After George's death, Helen was achingly lonesome. Even so, why marry Mike Davis? Her friends, and all of Denver, it seemed, kept asking. How could Helen Bonfils, major stockholder and secretary-treasurer of *The Denver Post*, Denver's Lady Bountiful, Broadway angel and actress, marry her much younger chauffeur?

In addition to why and how, they also persistently asked, in a truly meddlesome manner, where did this Mike Davis come from?

CHAPTER TWO

"It Still Seems Like a Fairy Story to Me"

Helen and Tiger Mike made an improbable pair, said people who saw their love affair firsthand. But it happened. And those who were there remember it from wildly conflicting perspectives. In their own words, they tell the story. Out of these reminiscences, a fuller picture emerges.

DAVE DAVIS
Brother

My brother, Michael Edward Davis, was born on a farm in Nebraska, the youngest of six children—four daughters and two sons—of Ella and Leo Lewis. I was the oldest son.

Our grandparents immigrated from Lebanon in the 1890s and were pioneer settlers in the Midwest. Our parents met and married in Nebraska.

The kids helped our father with the farm chores, slopping the pigs, milking the cows and driving the horse-drawn plow dad used before he purchased a tractor.

Later, Dad moved us to town. He owned a retail store and junk shop. Later, he also owned a dance hall and saloons. Our Dad was a helluva nice man. Our mother was kinda like Helen, she was always doing and giving for someone.

Eddie, as we called him then, wasn't too interested in school and he dropped out and went to work pounding ties on the railroad. Later, he was in the army. Then he came to Denver. That was about 1951, and he was in his early twenties.

SAMMY SUGARMAN
Owner, Shugie's Tavern

I've heard people say Mike was a dishwasher—or sometimes they'd say a fry cook—for a tavern on East Colfax Avenue before he became Miss Helen's chauffeur. They claimed to have seen him sweeping the sidewalk in front of the business. Well, I owned the business, a tavern, and I can tell you that a lot of that rags-to-riches story is bull. I'm Sammy Sugarman, former University of Denver football player, and was owner of the bar, Shugie's.

In his early days in Denver, in the late 1940s, Mike drove a cement truck. Nights, his favorite pasttime was to hang out at Shugie's. Shugie's was more than a run-of-the-neighborhood saloon. Not long before Mike appeared on the scene, I'd seen the comedians Tom and Dick Smothers at the Red Onion, a popular nightspot in Aspen. I had never laughed so hard. I booked the brothers for Shugie's and business was booming at the lounge.

I'm talking about the years from 1949 to 1953. There were an awful lot of rooming houses around, and after Mike rented a room in one of them, he became a customer. He would sit at the bar and order Canadian Club and ginger ale and sip one or two drinks all night.

He was a friendly kind of guy. He came in every night after work. At first, I had no idea what he did. It was a neighborhood tavern and everyone knew everyone else by first name. At one time there were a lot of nurses from nearby Presbyterian Hospital and men from Lowry Air Force Base. A lot of soldiers got married to a lot of nurses as a result.

When we closed at two, we used to go up the street to the Corner Kitchen, a twenty-four-hour place, for something to eat. Mike would come and have breakfast with us.

Since we had some good entertainment in the lounge, we were pretty busy. One Saturday night my barmaid didn't show up and we were swamped. Out of the blue this Mike Davis sitting at the bar said, "Mr. Sugarman, I can't stand to see you work so hard. Can't I wash the dishes?"

I said, "Man, you've got a job."

He was there every night when he got off work. He loved people. As I said, he had a job driving a cement truck and he came in sometimes in dusty clothes. He'd keep helping me and helping me. Maybe one of my workers wouldn't show up and he'd say, "Don't worry; I'll unload the beer, I'll stock the bar, sweep the sidewalk." Whatever. He'd do it.

I wanted to pay him, but he said, "I don't need your money. I've got a good job." I finally got his Social Security number and I think I paid him a total of one hundred dollars.

I guess this continued for three or four months. Weekends he'd stand at the front door and greet people. I think he wanted to be known as the owner, and that was all right with me. He was having a ball. He would have made a wonderful politician.

He brought his mother to Denver and she was a great Lebanese cook. She started sending me little cabbage sticks to take home to my wife. My wife had Mike to dinner. After one trip to Nebraska, Mike brought my wife a lamp; I think his family had a furniture store in Nebraska.

One night he comes and says, "Say, do you know a lady by the name of Helen Bonfils?"

I looked at him like he was crazy. I said I didn't know Helen Bonfils, but everyone knew of her. She was the owner of *The Denver Post*.

He said, "You'll never believe this, but I answered a blind ad and I got a job working for Helen Bonfils."

There, parked at the filling station across the street, was a big black Cadillac, a four-door. "This car belongs to her," he said. "I'm her chauffeur. She's married to a guy named George Somnes, and my job is just to take her out to Elitch's and bring her home."

Mike would come by a lot of times during the day and park in front. He always had a couple of dogs in the back seat. Nights when she was at Elitch's and she was ready for him to pick her up, she'd call and say, "Shugie, is Mike there?" And I'd say, "Yes, just a minute, Helen." She was a wonderful person.

He'd still help me out a lot after he was her chauffeur. I never saw him wear a uniform—maybe a driver's cap when he was in the car. He wore suits. He liked to get dressed up.

When she and George Somnes would fly to New York, he would drive the car back East so they would have it. He'd be gone from three to six weeks. Once he came back and said, "Here's a coat for you," and he gave me this nice cashmere coat. He would buy me expensive ties, shirts, lizard shoes, and purses for my wife. He used to come over to the house quite a bit.

He fell in love with one of the waitresses, a little red-headed girl with freckles. He would always bring her a box of candy. Everyone teased her and she would blush. It was just platonic.

One day he came in and said, "I'm still driving that black Cadillac for Helen Bonfils, but come see something."

I went across the street to the filling station with him, and there was a black Cadillac. "This one's mine," Mike said, and he showed me the ownership paper. He said Helen gave it to him.

I said, "You must be terrific in bed, Mike," and he kinda blushed.

Later, I began seeing these headlines in the newspapers about Davis striking oil. I couldn't believe what I read. I thought, well, maybe he is an oilman.

George Somnes died, and Helen and Mike married.

Then Mike started drilling oil wells like crazy and he was always getting his name in *The Denver Post*. The papers started calling him "Tiger Mike." Well, that summed him up. He had a tremendous office in the First National Bank Building in downtown Denver. My wife and I went with Lillian and Harry Hoffman (Denver's leading liquor dealer) to a Christmas party he gave there.

I could not believe what a fantastic office he had. And there was Helen Bonfils, just as gracious and on our level as could be. I said something two or three times like, "Boy, Mike, you must really be hung." I think it embarrassed him. Well, I was just putting two and two together. I figured why else would a woman like Helen Bonfils take up with Mike Davis?

His language was terrible. He thought it was cute. I think Helen liked hearing it; it was part of a life she'd never had before. I have a lot of dear memories of Mike. I never saw him smoke, never saw him take more than a sociable drink. He liked to buy drinks for the house. He had a filthy mouth, but he never used that language around my wife or kids.

I still saw Mike for a time after he became an oil man. He wore the ugliest pinstriped suits, just like a Mafia person. A friend of mine came back from Las Vegas and said, "Shugie, you'll never believe this! I was on the same plane going to Las Vegas as Mike Davis. He took me to the Flamingo Hotel for dinner, and you would have thought he owned the place." But, gradually, he disappeared from our lives. I thought we were friends, but I guess we were just acquaintances.

My friend, Leonard Alterman, who owned a furniture store next door, thought Mike was a pretty nice guy when he first came to Denver but that he sure got arrogant. Mike called Leonard after he was married and said he needed six bedroom sets for the servants' quarters. Leonard said, "Great, come in and look around."

Mike said, "You pick 'em out; it's your business."

Leonard said, "It was unbelievable. It's incredible that Helen Bonfils is interested in him. He isn't the smoothest, suavest person, you know."

It was interesting to see a man come to Denver from a little town in Nebraska, drive a cement truck, and marry Helen Bonfils. It still seems like a fairy story to me.

CHAPTER THREE

DENVER, 1895

Miss Helen always found children boring, so in deference to her lack of interest in the younger set, we will not inflict too many numbing details of her early years on the reader.

Suffice it to say, Frederick Bonfils brought his family to Denver in 1895, the year he and Harry Tammen took over *The Denver Post*. Bonfils had paid $12,000 for the newspaper. Tammen was his partner.

May, christened Mary Madeline, his eldest daughter, was born in Troy, New York, in 1883. There, Bonfils worked briefly for the *Troy News*. On assignment to cover the state fair, he was denied admittance because he had forgotten his press pass. He slugged the gatekeeper and went in to get his story.

Helen Gilmer Bonfils was born in Peekskill, New York, on November 26, 1889. By then, her father had completed a swath through Oklahoma that yielded him $15,000 from fraudulent land deals. He went on to prosper in equally phony lottery deals in Kansas City, Kansas. There, the problem seemed to be that no one ever collected the $15,000 prize for a winning lottery ticket that sold for one dollar.

Harry Tammen, left, and Frederick Bonfils were partners and devoted friends. They took over *The Denver Post* in 1895.

Courtesy of The Denver Post.

But now, in Denver, he was a newly respectable (for a time, at least) co-owner and publisher of *The Post*. May was twelve and Helen, six. Helen attended St. Mary's Academy and the Wolcott School for Girls, which were where all the best families of Denver sent their young ladies. Later, she followed May to the Brownell School in New York for "finishing."

Denver was only twenty-six years old when the Bonfils arrived, having been founded in 1859 by gold settlers on the banks of Cherry Creek. By the time the family was established in a proper brick home at 939 Corona Street, the city had a population of 130,000. In the family's early years in Denver, Fifteenth and Sixteenth Streets, the town's main thoroughfares, were often bogs of mud in the winter, and dusty, rutted roadways in the summer.

But, as Helen would come to appreciate, there were a number of impressive mansions, which had been recently built by silver barons; a Denver Club, where these mining nabobs could meet to congratulate and commiserate; two fine hotels, the Windsor and the Brown Palace; and several theaters, foremost among them the majestic Tabor Grand. Not long after the Bonfils arrived, Italian workmen began carving a splendid state capitol building out of granite on a bluff overlooking downtown. When it was completed, it would be topped by a gold dome and civic pride would soar as high as its shining apex, which was a mile high, plus.

However, at the time of the Bonfils' arrival, Denver was in the doldrums. Two years earlier, in 1893, a silver panic had wiped out the fortunes of many of the city's new millionaires, including that of the state's great benefactor, Horace Tabor. (He also kept tongues wagging because he divorced his loyal, hard-working wife, Augusta, to marry the much younger flibbertigibbet, Baby Doe.)

Still, *The Denver Post* prospered almost from the beginning. By 1901, it overtook the *Rocky Mountain News* in paid circulation, counting 24,213 readers to the *News*' 24,134. The *News* had labored nearly half a century to reach the 24,000 mark. *The Post* did it in fewer than six years.

The Post just kept growing as Bonfils and Tammen drove the proper people of Denver wild with their yellow journalism. The parents of May and Helen's classmates took *The Post*, but they had it delivered to the servants' entrance in back so no one would know.

In 1915, Bonfils purchased the fifty-room mansion that had been built by a wealthy Denver merchant, L.H. Guldman, owner of the Golden Eagle department store. The Guldman home had been the subject of reams of prose by overwrought society scribes ever since it was completed a few years earlier at East Tenth Avenue and Humboldt Street, just west of Cheesman Park. It was the showplace of the city, no doubt about it. It had one of the city's two indoor swimming pools (the other was in the mansion of brewer Verner Z. Reed). Guldman's three daughters entertained in the pool room's tiled expanse at morning plunge parties.

At night, a twenty-piece orchestra might play for galas in the ballroom. The banquet hall could seat 300 for early or late suppers. The Guldmans' guests sometimes included Mr. and Mrs. David May of St. Louis. (Mr. May's department store chain had grown from a general store at Leadville, Colorado.) There was a bowling alley and a billiard room, tennis courts, and stables stocked with horses for morning canters. In the summer, the Italian gardens were strung with colored lights for evening fetes.

All of Denver could read about these gala goings-on in the society columns. (In later years, it was alleged that *The Post* discriminated against Jews, but, if there was any truth to the charges, they never

The Bonfils mansion at Tenth and Humboldt had fifty rooms and an indoor swimming pool, and adjoined Cheesman Park.
Western History Collection, Denver Public Library.

applied to the Guldmans.) Of all the mansion's charms, Helen most yearned over the footlight-rimmed stage in the basement and its adjacent dressing room. There the Guldman daughters and their friends presented plays and tableaux for their appreciative audiences. Pretty Louise Guldman was a few years ahead of Helen at Wolcott School, and they became lifelong friends. Louise brought champagne to toast the Bonfils when they moved into her parents' former home.

There were persistent rumors that Bonfils had acquired the Guldman mansion by threatening to expose the family's son as a deviant. In the 1930s, lawyers from the *News* went over Bonfils' past with a fine-toothed comb as they prepared a defense against a libel charge Bonfils had brought against the paper. They couldn't find any evidence to support the blackmail story. In fact, Bonfils and Guldman were on friendly terms throughout their lifetimes and they entered into real estate transactions together in 1917 and 1926, as writer Bill Hosokawa related in his book about the early days of Denver's newspapers, *Thunder in the Rockies*.

F.G. Bonfils moved his family into the vast, marble-pillared mansion where music and laughter had filled the rooms and hallways, and silence descended. The lovely stage and dressing rooms Helen so yearned after gathered dust.

CHAPTER FOUR

The Grand Tour

When the time drew near for May to leave for Brownell College in New York, Frederick Bonfils found an excuse to postpone parting with his favorite daughter. He organized a half-year tour of Europe for the family, including his parents, Mr. and Mrs. Eugene Napoleon Bonfils.

Such a Grand Tour was de rigeur for people of any wealth and cultivation, and by 1902, seven years after arriving in Denver, Bonfils' circumstances were such that he qualified. (Though when it comes to culture, Bonfils was, after all, a not-quite-graduate of West Point with a nodding acquaintance of the classics.)

Such a lengthy trip abroad was novel enough to be newsworthy, especially when the traveler was F.G. Bonfils. So *The Denver Times* of January 31, 1902, saw fit to report that the Bonfils party would sail first to the Mediterranean "to enjoy the balmy breezes," and then "as the season advances…will proceed on their journey to France, Germany and Italy, proposing to be gone about six months."

Daughter May simply fell in love with the Old World, with the ruins of Greece and Rome, the beauty of Versailles and the art and architecture of Paris and London. The family visited Turkey and then entrained to Egypt, where May and Papa were photographed against a pyramid.

Helen and her father were more intrigued by the fauna of the countries they visited. In Paris, Papa paid an astronomical sum (one hundred dollars, he said) for a French poodle. Sadly, it didn't survive the trip home. Bonfils was talked out of bringing back some cobras, but he did succeed in importing a baboon from Egypt.

"He's about five feet high and as intelligent as some human beings," Papa told a reporter in Kansas City in June when he was interviewed on the way home to Denver.

"I am glad to get back to the United States," Bonfils said. "After visiting all the larger cities of Europe and taking trips to Cairo and Constantinople, I have come to the conclusion that Kansas City and Denver are the best cities in the world."

For Helen, the trip was the beginning and end of travels to faraway places. For one thing, in her later years she couldn't bring herself to get a passport because that would have meant revealing her true age. But May maintained she had found her spiritual home on the continent, and, later in life when she could afford to travel, she crossed the ocean on a number of trips.

CHAPTER FIVE

LIVING VICARIOUSLY

In the fall of 1903 May went off to finishing school.

Helen was, by turns, relieved and desolate: She was delighted to be the sole focus of her father's attentions. When Helen was very young, Papa would sometimes take May out to dinner, leaving Helen and his wife, Belle, at home. But, at first, Helen did miss May terribly. When the sisters were younger, May undoubtedly considered her little sister a pest sometimes, but they had grown to rely on each other for companionship because their father so restricted their social lives. Then, too, Denver was a very proper town, and many of the parents of their classmates at Wolcott School didn't approve of Papa and his scandal sheet.

"The Bonfils just aren't our kind," they might murmur to their daughters. Girls can be cruel, and such remarks got back to the family.

The other newspapers in town, the *Times*, the *Rocky Mountain News* and the *Denver Express* called Bonfils a blackmailer, a perjurer, a thief and a liar who did his business under aliases. The *Times* wrote that he might pose as a champion of the people now, but that he swindled the laboring classes of another state out of an enormous sum of money, and that he was escorted from Kansas City by the police department.

Papa's Girl

Actually, Bonfils had been a West Point cadet. He didn't graduate because he fell in love with Belle Barton, and, as he said, "You cannot at once be a bridegroom and a cadet." After that, he got caught up in the excitement of the Oklahoma Land Rush and, later, he was in land sales in Kansas City before the family moved to Denver.

Today Bonfils would be called a workaholic. Nights and Sundays he read and re-read *The Post*, furrowing his brow over what had been done or left undone. By 9:30 or 10:00 he was ready for bed, and so, as far as he was concerned, was the rest of his houshold.

F.G. Bonfils was very close with his money, but in one area he didn't stint: he was a dandy, favoring suits of a rather loud plaid. He was trim and erect and wore his clothes beautifully. Bonfils was, in a word, handsome.

Papa's nickel-nursing policies didn't extend to his family's wardrobes. May and Helen were always fashionably dressed, and the

Belle Bonfils was a serene presence in the volatile Bonfils household.
Courtesy of The Denver Post.

girls were permitted to order two hats apiece from Kate Feretti each season. Kate was a beguiling Italian woman who designed chapeaus for all of Denver's elite, including Molly Brown of Titanic fame.

May and Helen would visit Kate at her little Fifteenth Street shop. On their first visit, after their selections were complete, Kate asked in her Italian-flavored English if they planned to go to Baurs, the nearby restaurant where the ice cream soda had been invented.

"Oh, we don't have money for that," May demurred.

"You don't have money?" Kate cried in disbelief. "Your Papa's rich!"

The girls tried to explain Papa's theory of teaching them the value of a dollar. The upshot was Kate would make them two hats apiece and charge Papa more than their actual price. She gave the girls the difference for pocket money—a very satisfactory arrangement, they thought.

Holidays were lonely. On Christmas morning Helen and May opened a few practical presents. Mama and the girls would go to Mass and, afterwards, they would have dinner with Papa. Then he would shut himself up in the library with his work.

If life was on the dull side at home, Helen lived vicariously through *The Denver Post*. Thanks to Bonfils and Tammen and their wildly imaginative promotions chief, Al Birch, no one in Denver need be bored for long.

The *Post* building on Champa Street had an iron balcony on which Bonfils would frequently appear to toss pennies to the children below. Bonfils often paid people to do stunts. Once, the great Harry Houdini attached a rope to that same balcony and hung by his heels while escaping from a straitjacket. Another time, Bonfils invited local girls to grapple with a troupe of women wrestlers.

The Post was one of the first newspapers to install an electric scoreboard on the street for the World Series. Hundreds of Denverites would gather outside the building to follow the games.

Crowds filled the streets as well to watch "human flies" scale the sides of the Foster Building across the street. Or a turnip might be tossed from that building's twelfth floor and caught on a fork which the vaudevillian Gene Bedini held in his mouth.

And there were treasure hunts and prizes for the largest trout caught in Colorado waters, awards for the best shaped foot,

F.G. liked promotions and stunts, and pretty girls. Here he is with Miss Frontier Days and her attendant.
Courtesy of The Denver Post.

handsomest back, the oldest married couple, best kids' rodeo costume, best horseshoe pitcher, finest lawns and gardens, and much more. There was always something going on at *The Post*. And Papa made it happen!

Bonfils met all the celebrities who passed through Denver, and he and his chauffeur would frequently take them on sight-seeing trips in the mountains.

The publisher met with the evangelist Billy Sunday; he charmed Queen Marie of Rumania, as he inevitably charmed women; and chatted with the famous lawyer Clarence Darrow. Then there were the top comic strip artists: Sidney Smith, who drew Andy Gump; George McManus of Jiggs; and, best of all, Harold Gray, who created Little Orphan Annie.

Not one of the snooty girls at Wolcott School had a father like F.G. Bonfils!

Papa's Girl

But something happened when Helen was fourteen, something she was never supposed to know about. Papa fell in love.

The object of his affections was Mrs. Madge Reynolds, a Denver socialite, who went to *The Post* to ask Bonfils for help in her crusade to free Antone Wood, a ten-year-old boy convicted of murdering his adult hunting companion for his pocket watch.

The two met in February 1903, when Bonfils was forty-three and "Mrs. Reynolds was in her full blown thirties, slender, with deep gold hair and large, violet eyes," Gene Fowler wrote in *Timberline*.

After an hour-long conversation in Bonfils' office about Wood, and after Madge had departed, Papa remarked admiringly to his partner, Harry Tammen, "That woman has the biggest heart in the world."

Soon there were frequent meetings in Bonfils' office regarding Antone Wood. Before long, Bonfils and Mrs. Reynolds were riding horseback together, and he became a caller at her Logan Street home. She welcomed him evenings in the cozy breakfast nook where they shared the cakes she baked herself and half-pint bottles of champagne (although Bonfils was not a drinker, he did allow himself an occasional glass of champagne.)

"And so the months passed," Fowler wrote in *Timberline*. "Bonfils began to call her 'Dearest.' Their idyll was accepted by nearly everyone as a thing of sentimental beauty, an association rather than an amour."

This was surprisingly tactful of Fowler; Helen later learned that her father and Mrs. Reynolds were said to have had a love child. This girl, Betty Craig, grew up to be *The Post*'s drama editor, and her position was guaranteed for life.

By 1908, Bonfils was holding conversations with his friend and partner about a hypothetical case in which a rich and powerful man gave up everything "to wander hand in hand with a beautiful and understanding woman."

And Mr. Tammen supposedly replied, "Well, come out of the ether and think it over first."

On the afternoon of February 21, 1908, Bonfils and Mrs. Reynolds went riding. He came to his office the next morning and picked up the *Rocky Mountain News*.

Two *Post* staffers, passing the door of Bonfils' office, heard a moan. Fowler wrote: "They looked in and saw Bonfils standing there, his knees buckling, his eyes staring. Then he fell to the floor senseless, the newspaper beside him. Its headline read: Mrs. Reynolds Dies."

After a horseback ride, it was said, she had gone home, changed from her riding habit to a dressing gown, then dropped dead. The death certificate, signed by Dr. O.H. Pfeiffer, listed angina pectoris as the cause of death. Madge's funeral took place in her home on Logan Street. Bonfils was not among the prominent Denverites named as pallbearers.

At the cemetery he watched from a distance as his hated enemies—Senator Patterson; William "Napoleon" Evans, the powerful utilities magnate; and Thomas J. O'Donnell, corporation attorney—placed the coffin on a lowering device. As the casket vanished beneath the level of the cemetery lawn, Bonfils suddenly left his place in the background, Fowler wrote.

"His bare head was held high, almost defiantly so. He passed through the ranks of mourners. He stooped to pluck a single flower from his blanket of red roses. He straightened quickly, stepped nearer to the grave, leaned over it, and with a slow movement of the hand, dropped the rose on the lid of the casket.

"Then he strode rapidly to his automobile, staring straight ahead. He stepped inside and the chauffeur closed the door. He had said farewell in the presence of his enemies."

That was Papa, Helen would have said.

CHAPTER SIX
MAY ELOPES

May completed finishing school at Brownell College in the usual two years. On the spring morning after her return to Denver, the family gathered for breakfast.

We can imagine the scene at this happy family reunion, Papa beaming at May, and Mama giving her fond pats. And, knowing Helen's jealous nature, we can suspect that Helen must have seethed at this shower of attention. After all, she must have reasoned, they did have another daughter, one who had been keeping them company the last two years.

Helen would have had to admit, however, that May was looking lovely with her masses of golden hair and deep blue eyes, her porcelain complexion, and that heart-shaped face. It was almost unfair that she had a curvaceous figure to boot. The sisters had the same coloration, but Helen must have felt quite dumpy by comparison in her somewhat pudgy fifteen-year-old body.

Of course, May was aglow, basking in all the attention. She announced, "I'm going to a dance tonight, to celebrate my birthday."

"Oh," Papa said, obviously disappointed, "I thought you'd want to spend the evening with me—with your family."

"But, Papa!" May exclaimed, "It's my birthday. I'm twenty-one!"

"You don't love me or else you wouldn't want to go out. You can only go out only if you take me with you," Papa said stiffly.

May went to the dance—and Bonfils went with her.

It wasn't lost on the fellows of Denver that May was a stunner, and Helen must have felt twinges of envy when she saw how men reacted to her older sister, their heads swiveling wildly when she passed by. One in particular, Clyde V. Berryman, who worked at Wells Music as a piano salesman, was smitten. That summer of 1904, May seemed to take a great interest in the piano. This required a lot of trips downtown on the streetcar to buy sheet music. Usually, Helen went along.

Clyde was good-looking in a rangy, long-faced sort of way. Helen observed that he always made sure he was the one to wait on May, and he was quite fresh with her, Helen thought.

"I'm sure you have just the touch for this one," Clyde might say, offering May the sheet music for a Chopin sonata. "Though I don't know as much about your touch as I'd like to." May would blush and look at him sideways, and they would smile at each other while he rang up the sale.

She was stuck on him, it was plain to see. And he thought she was the cat's pajamas, in the parlance of the day.

Still, Helen was surprised when May swore her to secrecy and confessed that she was slipping out her bedroom window at night to meet Clyde to go walking in Cheesman Park, a beautiful big park that adjoined the grounds of the Bonfils' mansion.

Actually, May didn't have much choice. Papa wouldn't let her date unless he first approved the fellow, and it didn't seem likely he would look favorably on a sheet music salesman. No, Clyde Berryman wouldn't have been at all acceptable to Papa.

What May was doing was exciting and scary and we can imagine that Helen begged her for details.

"What do you do in the park?"

"Oh, we walk and...we sit and spoon..."

But Helen would have wanted to know more: about the kisses and embraces, and what did he do with his hands? Earthy from an early age, by this time Helen had learned some of the facts of life.

Papa's Girl

May Bonfils Berryman, sometime after her first marriage in 1904.
Courtesy of The Denver Post.

She and her best friend, Selma Groth, had traveled with the Sells Floto Circus—which Bonfils and Tammen owned—the summer before. Selma's father, Louis Groth, was the circus manager.

But, "no, that's enough," May would have said, and smiled her secret smile.

Not too much later, on November 7, 1904, on a day when Papa was out of town, May and Clyde eloped to Golden and were married in a civil ceremony.

When Bonfils was told, we can assume he turned livid. Married! Who had she married? A sheet music salesman? Had May lost her mind? Where did the fellow come from?

From Nebraska, May would have said. Clyde's father was a pioneer merchant of the state, she might have added with as much bravado as she could muster.

"A merchant? Is he a Catholic?"

"No, Papa," May would have had to admit. At this, Mama, who was devout, must have blanched. (Papa didn't become a convert until his death.) "But, Papa," May would have wheedled, "we're in love."

"In love!" Papa would have spat out the words. "Good Lord, girl, how can you be so gullible? The fellow's a fortune hunter plain and simple. It's my money he's after."

"How does this whipper-snapper propose to support you?" would have been Papa's next question. "Can he give you the kind of life you're used to?" indicating the marble-floored entry way, the great curving stairway in the hall, the frescoed ceilings, the masses of dark mahogany furniture, and beyond all this, the grounds and gardens, the tennis courts, the garage and, over it, the servants' quarters.

"He has a position…" May might have offered.

"Hah!" Papa would have snorted. "I'll tell you what he proposes to do. He intends for me to support him! Well, I won't have it."

Papa said this was May's home, and she would always be welcome, but he would never accept her husband as his son-in-law. Never. He was icy cold.

May said that she would leave and asked that her clothes be sent to her.

"No," Bonfils said. "I will not send your clothes to you."

Helen and Mama followed May to her room and, weeping, helped her pack a suitcase. Of course, Helen wanted to ask about her wedding night. What had happened when they turned out the lights? But clearly this wasn't the time.

Papa stormed off to walk in the park.

May and Clyde left Denver. They led a wandering existence that took them to Kansas City for a time, then Omaha, where Clyde sold pianos for about seven years. They moved on to California, to Oakland and Los Angeles. Mama and Helen visited them several times during those years, staying for several weeks at a time. Mama sent May money quite regularly, and sometimes Papa even wrote her an affectionate letter. But he never relaxed his resolve not to accept Clyde as a son-in-law.

The young couple returned to Denver about 1916 and took a room at the Hotel Hesse at East Colfax Avenue and Grant Street.

Papa's Girl

At a distance, May and her "poor excuse for a husband" had been a disappointment to Papa, but as lodgers in a cheap hotel in Denver, they were an embarrassment.

Since Clyde obviously couldn't do any better by his daughter, Papa helped Clyde purchase a two-story brick home at 1129 Lafayette Street. It was quite an acceptable address. Just four blocks away, at more fashionable 750 Lafayette Street, off stately East Seventh Avenue, lived the John S. Douds, and their daughter, Mamie. That same year, 1916, she married a young lieutenant, Dwight D. Eisenhower.

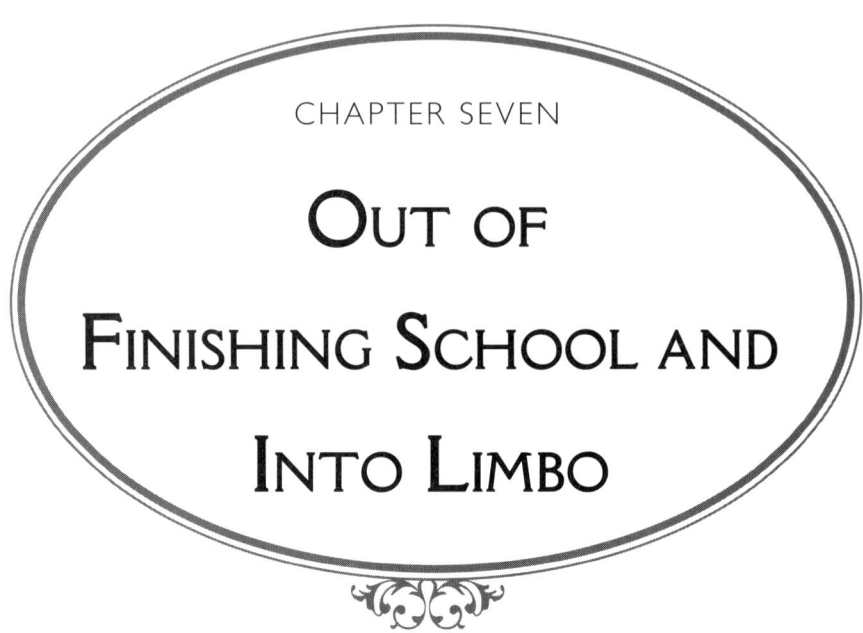

CHAPTER SEVEN
Out of Finishing School and Into Limbo

In 1909, Helen went off to New York, to Brownell College, the same finishing school May had attended. Among the subjects she studied was elocution. "Papa always said a pleasant speaking voice is important in a woman," she told friends. If he had known how his daughter would eventually put those mellifluous accents to use—as an actress—he would regret ever having mentioned the accomplishment.

And then she returned to Denver. Life became a round of shopping with Mama and occasional trips to New York; of playing bridge with her girlfriends and going to the theater with Mama, Papa, and the Tammens.

Denver was a wonderful theater town in those days. Live theater flourished at the Denver Auditorium, the Tabor Grand, and the Broadway. Selma and Helen never missed the Saturday matinee at Elitch's.

Bonfils and Tammen bought the Empress Theatre, and their families saw such stars as Charles Chaplin and Stan Laurel on the Pantages Vaudeville Circuit.

In June 1913, Helen drove her Fritchie electric car in an auto contest for women from Denver to Mount Morrison, a trip of some

Papa's Girl

Helen presented a jaunty appearance as she posed in her car with a tiger cub from the Sells-Floto Circus.
Courtesy of The Denver Post.

seventeen miles. Selma and Helen tooled around Denver in Helen's auto, sometimes with a lion cub which Papa had given her for her birthday.

HELEN BLACK
Co-Founder, Denver Symphony Orchestra

I used to go back to New York to engage artists to appear with the orchestra. One day I was in the Denver & Rio Grande railway office when Helen and her mother were getting their tickets for a trip to New York. They wanted to take a compartment, but Helen's father said they had to purchase berths, and they were trying to think of a way to get around him.

Ella Sullivan was *The Post*'s society editor and a real power in the town. Helen's father wanted Helen to be in the Denver Country Club but the club wouldn't accept the Bonfils. Finally, the board of directors gave in because of Ella's persuasions. But I don't think Helen ever went there because she knew she would be kept at arm's length.

The Bonfils joined the Lakewood Country Club, one of the area's new clubs, and Helen took up golf for a while. But, as she told me, "Darling, I was never athletic."

DR. OSGOOD PHILPOTT
Denver Dermatologist

I first met Miss Helen, as Helen Bonfils was known even then, when she was in her early twenties. I had recently graduated from the University of Colorado Medical School, and had found a promising position as assistant to Dr. A.J. Markley, dean of dermatology at the school.

Dr. Markley and his wife were untiring social climbers. First thing in the morning, they read the newspaper's social column.

Since the Bonfils had no social standing due to Mr. Bonfils' reputation as the publisher of a scandal sheet, Mrs. Bonfils was assigned to me when she called for an appointment. I found Belle Bonfils to be a very repressed person. She had a few skin problems that brought her to me.

Her husband, F.G. Bonfils, was considered to be quite a flashy man who took advantage of every situation he could. He was a fascinating man, but a very dominating personality.

Mrs. Bonfils brought Helen to me with a skin complaint. Helen was a very kind, interested person. She made you feel you were the most important person in the world.

It was well known that Frederick Bonfils kept a tight rein on his daughter. A friend of mine, Clarence Cobb, was a young, unmarried, fashionable blade, always in demand as a partner at dinner or to make a fourth at bridge. Cobbie met Helen and tried at least a dozen times to get a date. She would always say, "Thank you, Mr. Cobb. I will let you know in the morning." He would call and she would always say she was sorry, but she couldn't go out with him.

For a year he kept trying, because he thought she was fascinating. Finally, one morning when he called, she said she could see him. He called for her at the mansion. He rang the bell at about

Frederick G. Bonfils in his office.

eight and saw someone peering out the window, and out came Mr. Bonfils himself.

Clarence said, "I have come to call for Helen."

"Yes," said F.G. "I want to talk to you first. Helen has to be back on this porch at a quarter to twelve, and if she isn't, you'll hear from me."

During the evening, Clarence said to Helen, "I've asked you a dozen times to go out and you never agreed. How did it happen that you did tonight?"

"I have to get permission from my father," Helen said. "He always said you were too flashy, but this time he changed his mind."

Cobbie said many years later that it was too bad she didn't have the same freedom as other girls. She wouldn't have picked such lemons as husbands.

The first time Mrs. Bonfils and Helen came to my office after Bonfils' death, I extended my condolences. "I'm sure you will miss him," I said.

"Miss him!" Mrs. Bonfils said. "If you had to crawl out of bed over two shotguns and light a fire in the fireplace every morning, you'd know how much I miss him!"

I doubt if anyone ever paid much attention to Mrs. Bonfils. She was very meek, very mild, and I was surprised when she expressed herself as violently as she did. It was entirely out of character.

BERNADINE KIRCHOF
Girlhood Friend

We lived about a block from Helen and we often played bridge together. I remember one time when we were at Helen's house, one of the girls was wearing something very becoming and we were all exclaiming over how pretty she looked. Helen didn't like that one bit. She always had the latest thing, and she liked to be the center of attention.

I don't think Helen had a date until she was past twenty. I know my brother and some of his friends decided to go calling and old F.G. kicked them out.

Since Papa was so strict about Helen's dating, she decided there was nothing for it but to follow May's example and slip out of her bedroom window occasionally to meet a beau. Friends recall her mentioning, in later years, a poet, and a fellow who became a Denver psychiatrist. Her friend and physician, Dr. Frank McGlone, said Helen told him she was in love with a doctor with Denver's Department of Health and Hospitals. Bonfils nixed that romance because the man was Jewish. But Helen remembered all too well Papa's cold fury when May followed her foolish heart and eloped, so she was much more circumspect. She waited until he was out of town on fishing or business trips to slide out of her window and into the arms of her waiting swains.

Thus, time went on, uneventfully for the most part, until Helen was thirty. That year, a man who would be her friend and confidante for the next thirty years joined the Bonfils' household staff.

Papa's Girl

ROBERT STOUFFER
Chauffeur

When I arrived in Denver in 1919 it had the likeness of a frontier town. It was common to see gun-toting cowboys, miners, ranchers and western characters strolling the streets. A mile above sea level and close to the Rocky Mountains, the air was clear and rarefied. The state capitol building with its gold-covered dome presented a striking picture. Fine large mansions with spacious grounds bore proof of well-to-do families.

The wealthier people banded together to keep wages at a minimum. Girls working in stores and offices were paid from six to nine dollars a week. If they complained of not being able to live on that, they were told to get themselves a man. Money controlled the town and those who had it were averse to having the working man enjoy the privileges that they could afford. Anyone who attempted to unionize workers was promptly arrested as a vagrant and given twenty-four hours to leave town.

I had been gassed during World War I and I had left my native New Jersey to find a job in the West. Wishing to be out-of-doors as much as possible, I took a job as chauffeur for F.G. Bonfils. A Jersey City doctor had taught me to drive, first a Ford, then a Studebaker, so I was able to drive him about.

(Robert Stouffer proved to be an excellent mechanic who kept a fleet of cars, including Belle's ancient electric, in good repair. Investors, both crackpot and plausible, often brought their motorized contraptions to the wealthy publisher. Bonfils, who considered his chauffeur a mechanical whiz, would turn their work over to Stouffer for testing.)

Bonfils had come to Denver with some money. Tammen had a small curio store and had been bartender at the Windsor Hotel. Their other enterprises included a coal business, a circus, a weekly farm paper, *The Great Divide,* the *Kansas City Post,* two vaudeville theaters and several land development projects.

F.G. Bonfils was a well-built, good-looking man, five feet eight and one-half inches tall. His hair was bushy and dark brown. A pointed, waxed moustache gave him a French look. His blue-gray piercing eyes were capable of expressing both pleasure and anger. Several years at West Point had given him a military bearing.

Papa's Girl

There was a marked difference in his attitude toward those he liked and who agreed with him and his policies, than toward those who incurred his displeasure and upon whom he waged unrelenting warfare.

A naturalist and an animal lover, he always gave the game a fair chance. Many times I witnessed him gently remove his hook from an undersized fish and after kissing it, return it to the water. Or, when a fish had put up a good fight, he would set it free.

He had a photographic eye and was prone to make snap judgments which, once made, were seldom altered. His ambition was to acquire money and power. Almost to the point of miserliness, he regarded any expenditure as representing the interest on so much money. A hard loser, he could not stand anyone getting the lion's share. It was said that his Wall Street rating was sixty million, and that he could raise a million cash any day.

The Bonfils home was a large mansion on property that extended over half a block and adjoined a lovely park. The interior was lavishly furnished and decorated with Napoleon-period effects throughout. In it were a conservatory, pool room, swimming pool, entertainment room (with stage), wine cellar, and so forth. On the grounds were a large garage, tennis court, fountain, flower beds, trees and lawn. I was to live in a five-room furnished apartment above the garage.

Nobody used the tennis court at the Bonfils home so I turned it into a vegetable garden. In time I was assigned the supervision of the place, planning the flower beds, hiring maintenance men and making repair contracts. F.G. always kept several dogs, either as pets or for hunting. Mrs. Bonfils had a number of birds, canaries, linnets, love birds and one cardinal.

I was twenty-four years of age, having been born February 27, 1896, in the East Liberty Section of Pittsburgh, Pennsylvania. I was younger than either May or Helen, who were then thirty-seven and thirty-one, respectively. May was married and lived in a modest home several blocks away. Two of F.G.'s brothers, Tom and Charlie, lived at the (Bonfils) home. Tom was clerk of the county court and Charlie a proofreader at *The Post*.

Both Mrs. Bonfils and Helen were very attentive to me—would see that my bedding was changed every week and try to make things pleasant for me. My work was not difficult. I'd often go on fishing or hunting trips with F.G.

Many persons of prominence visited *The Post* and Mr. Bonfils and I were given the job of taking them on sight-seeing trips or fishing: Jack Dempsey, Will Rogers.

Other guests who came to Denver were Amelia Earhart; Damon Runyon, who had worked for *The Post* and was now a New York columnist; Mary Pickford and Douglas Fairbanks; and John Philip Sousa. Helen was fascinated by our contacts with these famous visitors and often probed F.G. and me for details about them.

F.G. insisted I accompany Mrs. Bonfils and Helen when they went out in the evening. I always felt self-conscious at these times for I would be treated as one of the party. Denver's high society set

F.G. welcomed Amelia Earhart to Denver after her solo flight across the Atlantic in 1932.
Courtesy of The Denver Post.

didn't accept Mrs. B. or the daughters into their ranks until years later. However, Helen belonged to the Junior League, and both Mrs. B. and Helen were members of the Social Center and Day Nursery, an institution that cared for children of poor families when mothers were at work. Funds for operation were obtained from the sale of contributed articles of clothing, books, pictures, and so forth at a store located downtown. I'd often help them at the store as well as aid in preparing and distributing Christmas and Thanksgiving baskets. I also aided in purchasing and wrapping presents for the children.

Several times when I donned an outfit and played Santa to over one hundred kids, a *Post* photographer would take my picture and it would appear in the paper. It was at one of these affairs that I met Anna Roybal, a young Spanish widow who had two small boys. After a courtship, we were married. Anna wanted one of the boys, Donald, to become a priest, so he was receiving training at a Catholic institution. The other boy, Tommy, lived and was raised with us. In April 1926, our daughter, Ann Elizabeth, or Betty, as we called her, was born.

Tom and Betty could not have much freedom, because we lived on someone else's property, but Cheesman Park next door afforded them ample playgrounds. When I could leave my work, we went on picnic trips, drives, and to shows. I had passes to all the shows. The circus usually showed in Canada before coming to Denver. The crew would smuggle in Canadian whiskey, hiding it under the animal cages, and would usually give me a few bottles. May B. would invariably talk me out of the whiskey, saying it was the only thing that would relieve her headaches.

In the early 1920s, a Dr. Locke organized the Ku Klux Klan in Denver. Listed in its membership were many public officials ranging from governor down to members of the police force. *The Post* repeatedly denounced the KKK in editorials, pointing out that it was a sad state of affairs when law enforcement officers would become members of such a secret organization. There were several demonstrations in which fiery crosses were burned in front of *The Post* and also on the lawns of the Bonfils and Tammen homes. *The Post* kept up its fight and eventually the KKK was disbanded.

Papa's Girl

We'd repeatedly get warnings that some person or gang was out to kill F.G., so I had been instructed to carry a gun at all times. We had several close calls but that was it.

F.G. Bonfils had good reason to fear for his life.

Early in the 1900s there was a shootout in the office Bonfils shared with Tammen at *The Post*. The details were these:

An attorney, W. W. "Plug Hat" Anderson, burst into the room to confront *The Post* owners over their refusal to pay his fee for helping to obtain a pardon for Alferd Packer, the so-called "man-eater" tried and imprisoned for having slain and eaten five prospectors in the blizzard of 1873 outside Lake City, near Gunnison. Anderson fired at Bonfils and the bullet passed through his shoulder and ploughed upward through his throat. A second shot grazed his heart. Anderson fired twice at Tammen, shattering his wrist and furrowing his shoulder. Reporters crowded around the doorway into the City Room, but they appeared paralyzed with shock. Reporter Polly Pry, who had written the series of articles which led to Packer's pardon by the governor, was in the office. She became the heroine of the scenario when she grappled with Anderson and seized his pistol.

And that is how F.G.'s office at *The Denver Post* came to be known as "The Bucket of Blood."

Helen was still a child at the time, but she always remembered how slow and painful Papa's recovery was, and how concerned she and Mama were for him.

CHAPTER EIGHT
TWO CHILDHOODS

TOM STOUFFER
Chauffeur's Son

I lived with my mother and father in the apartment over the Bonfils' garage from the time I was seven or eight until I went to college in 1938. I enjoyed it, but I had to know my place. I played around the lower part of the yard with my friends from across the street, and the whole of Cheesman Park was also our playground.

 Good old F.G. was a very distinguished man, very outgoing. He was a good-looking man with a moustache he kept kind of waxed. When my friends and I played baseball or softball in Cheesman Park and he was out walking the dogs, he would stop and watch. He did an awful lot of fishing, often at the Wigwam Club above Deckers, and I used to look forward to his coming home with my Dad with a big string of fish. One time Mr. Bonfils and my Dad took me to a little stream near Littleton. We caught some brook trout and Dad built a fire and cooked over it.

 Miss Helen was a very good-looking woman and she was friendly. She showed off her voluptuous figure. She played the piano, and I would hear her playing or sometimes singing on the upstairs balcony over the driveway, both popular and classical music. She was a very gifted woman with a very nice voice.

Helen had gentlemen friends who would visit when F.G. was not there. One I recall vividly, a doctor in an army uniform with riding britches and shiny boots. They made quite a couple, walking in the lower part of the yard to the vine-covered arbor, holding hands.

As chauffeur, Dad would drive three autos, a Franklin, a Pierce Arrow, and a Packard. He was a master mechanic as well as a jack of all trades. Belle Bonfils had an electric automobile, a strange contraption. She would use it to visit friends in the neighborhood, looking very stately. She was very friendly and always spoke to me. She was plain, but a proud woman, somehow distinguished. She and Helen and F.G. got along real well with each other, and with Charlie and Tom, too.

Helen in her younger years was "a Marilyn Monroe type," according to one admirer. *Courtesy of* The Denver Post.

May lived three or four blocks away, and she would come visit. Her husband never came unless F.G. was gone. May was a good-looking woman, too, but not as flamboyant as Helen, who you could characterize as a Marilyn Monroe type. She liked to get attention; May was the other way, not as outgoing.

Helen married Mr. Somnes after her father's death. Somnes was a wishy-washy type of individual, one we would call a wimp in the vernacular of today. I thought he tried to act the big wheel, but he was no more one than I was.

My brother, Donny, had been placed in an orphanage at the north end of town. My father and mother had to arrange that because the Bonfils wanted only one child on the property. We used to go to visit him, and my parents told me he was my cousin. I never knew I had a brother until I was in the service, and it came out when the army was doing a background check on me.

I had a job taking care of the lawn at the mansion for fifty dollars a month, and Mr. Bonfils paid part of my tuition to Colorado College. I joined the service in 1943 at Fort Lupton. I stayed in the service twenty-six and one-half years and retired as a Master Sergeant. I was married in 1949 in Germany. We got remarried by a justice of the peace in Denver and Helen stood up for us.

BETTY ONDRUSEK-MEYER
Chauffeur's Daughter

In 1925, when my father had to tell Mr. and Mrs. Bonfils that my mother was pregnant (with me), it was a real dilemma. It had been upsetting enough—to the Bonfils—several years before when he had told them he wished to marry Anna Roybal, a widow with two young sons.

They solved that inconvenience by agreeing that one son, Tommy, would be allowed to live in the garage apartment with his parents while the other was sent away. Tommy was a charmer. His younger brother, Donny, was shy and his face was disfigured by Smallpox scars. Supposedly he was preparing for the priesthood, but that never came to pass.

And, now, there was to be another child.

So, it was with some trepidation that father went to Mr. and Mrs. Bonfils to tell them the news. Well, my father had made himself almost indispensable to the household during his six years of employment, so they agreed that he could stay. But they said the new child must be kept out of sight at all times.

I don't know how the Bonfils expected my mother and father to avoid having any more children, but for my parents the answer was abstinence. I slept with my mother.

I grew up nearly invisible on the grounds, ducking around corners and hiding behind hedges when I heard the limousine approaching on the driveway. In many ways it was a lonely life. I attended school with children who, for the most part, came from the big homes in the neighborhood. Many of them were delivered to school by limousine. I had two dresses my mother made for school, and a third one for Sundays.

On Fridays there was often a lot of excited chatter among my schoolmates about the birthday party they would all be attending on Saturday. I had a lot of friends, but I was never invited to their parties. When I screwed up the courage to ask why, I was told that I couldn't be invited because I was the child of a servant. I always felt the outsider as the daughter of the Bonfils' chauffeur.

My mother was my salvation. Nights when she put my hair up in rag curlers, she would reassure me, "Remember, mi amor, you are just as good as anyone."

And my father would say, "You are not better than anyone else, but you are just as good."

One time, after Miss Helen married George Somnes, he heard me singing in our apartment over the garage. He asked my father who was singing and commented that "a voice like that could go far in New York." But I can't say there was a fairy-story ending with me on Broadway. Actually, I made my career with the Jefferson County Schools, in the purchasing department.

Sometimes, when the Bonfils' family was away, I would go with my father to check on the mansion before he went to bed. I would follow him through the house in the dark as his flashlight searched out the corners. So I became familiar with the rooms and the massive furnishings.

Miss Helen was my godmother, and I still wear the little gold cross she gave me when I was baptized. When I was older, she would acknowledege my existence and would remember me at Christmas with a piece of jewelry, just junk jewelry, actually.

May was a nicer, warmer person, from my viewpoint. She was more natural; she didn't wear makeup. Helen had sheer triangles of fabric affixed to the corners of her eyes and mouth to pull them tight. And she would wear heavy makeup to cover these.

I learned from my father that Helen tried to come on to him a number of times, but he would have nothing to do with that. He was very straight and proper.

CHAPTER NINE
THRENODY

Harry Tammen died of cancer on July 19, 1924. Bonfils wept, the first time anyone had ever seen him cry. Almost thirty years before, they had become partners with the shake of a hand. They never had a contract. Bonfils said, "More than half of me has gone. I shall never get over it, for Harry and I were so necessary to each other."

They had built the little *Evening Post* into Colorado's mightiest newspaper. Its circulation of 161,000 daily—close to 240,000 on Sunday—was twice that of its three rivals, the *Express*, *Times* and *News* combined.

ROBERT STOUFFER
Chauffeur

In January of 1933, F.G. contracted a bad cold. On his last day downtown, Thursday, January 26, he extracted his will from his bank safety deposit box. He told me that he was going to make some changes in it, one of which would ensure me of substantial renumeration for the rest of his life. He pigeonholed the will in his desk with the intention of codiciling it the following day. He never got to make the changes. One of the last things he said to me was, "Son, we're going to have good times from now on. We'll just let others worry about the business. We'll make the North Platte fishing trip each year even if you and I go alone."

He begged me to help him get dressed to go to *The Post*. Said he wanted to get his will changed. Then he went into a coma from which he never awakened. Early Thursday morning, February 2, 1933, F.G. died of what was described as toxic encephalitis, an acute inflammation of the brain. He was seventy-two years old. That afternoon *The Post* devoted almost six pages to the news of his death. "Colorado Has Lost Its Greatest Citizen" read the large headline on Page One, enclosed in a black border.

I must say that without the efforts of able and loyal employees, *The Post* would not have been successful. Though grossly underpaid, none of the employees benefited in either Tammen's or F.G.'s wills. Some had grown old in their years of faithful service. How inconsistent with one of *The Post*'s boasts: "Oh, Justice, when expelled from other habitations, make this thy dwelling place."

The funeral took place on a Saturday, and as Mrs. Tammen had been in California and couldn't get to Denver until Sunday, the interment and sealing of the crypt was delayed until her arrival. The casket was kept under guard at the house until the following Monday, when I was asked by Mrs. Bonfils and Helen to take a final view of F.G.'s remains and supervise the crypt interment. The saddest part of my duty was to be present at the embalming, and to advise the morticians as to makeup, etc.

During the time F.G. lay on his deathbed, Denver millionaire Charlie Boettcher was kidnapped and held captive in South Dakota until a substantial ransom was paid. His captors, who were later apprehended, said their original plan had been to kidnap F.G. They said that they knew that F.G. and I usually took an after-dinner stroll in Cheesman Park. They said that if I had interfered they would have just bumped me off. F.G.'s sickness prevented their carrying out their plans. F.G. had a premonition that such an event might occur and had warned me several times that if we were accosted, to not hesitate to shoot.

In spite of F.G.'s shortcomings, I had a deep regard for him and I know that he thought a lot of me. He was extremely courteous to womenfolk, and when any irregularities involving office girls irritated him, he'd often vent his displeasure on me. On several such occasions I threatened to quit, but he'd pacify me with an explanation and a raise in pay, telling me not to pay any attention to him.

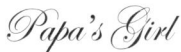

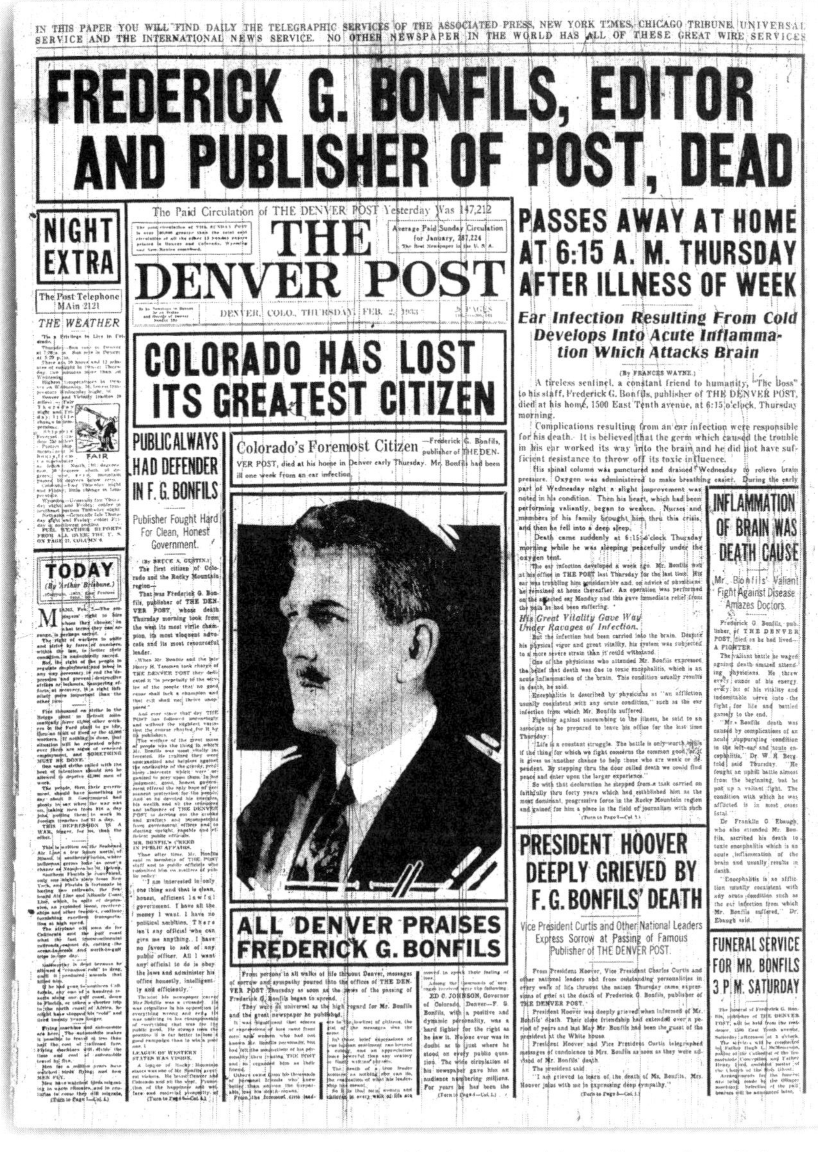

IN THIS PAPER YOU WILL FIND DAILY THE TELEGRAPHIC SERVICES OF THE ASSOCIATED PRESS, NEW YORK TIMES, CHICAGO TRIBUNE, UNIVERSAL SERVICE AND THE INTERNATIONAL NEWS SERVICE. NO OTHER NEWSPAPER IN THE WORLD HAS ALL OF THESE GREAT WIRE SERVICES

FREDERICK G. BONFILS, EDITOR AND PUBLISHER OF POST, DEAD

NIGHT EXTRA

The Post Telephone MAin 2121

The Paid Circulation of THE DENVER POST Yesterday Was 147,212

Average Paid Sunday Circulation for January, 287,224
The Best Newspaper in the U. S. A.

THE DENVER POST

DENVER, COLO., THURSDAY, FEB. 2, 1933

PASSES AWAY AT HOME AT 6:15 A. M. THURSDAY AFTER ILLNESS OF WEEK

Ear Infection Resulting From Cold Develops Into Acute Inflammation Which Attacks Brain

(By FRANCES WAYNE.)

A tireless sentinel, a constant friend to humanity, "The Boss" to his staff, Frederick G. Bonfils, publisher of THE DENVER POST, died at his home, 1500 East Tenth avenue, at 6:15 o'clock, Thursday morning.

Complications resulting from an ear infection were responsible for his death. It is believed that the germ which caused the trouble in his ear worked its way into the brain and he did not have sufficient resistance to throw off its toxic influence.

His spinal column was punctured and drained Wednesday to relieve brain pressure. Oxygen was administered to make breathing easier. During the early part of Wednesday night a slight improvement was noted in his condition. Then his heart, which had been performing valiantly, began to weaken. Nurses and members of his family brought him thru this crisis, and then he fell into a deep sleep.

Death came suddenly at 6:15 o'clock Thursday morning while he was sleeping peacefully under the oxygen tent.

COLORADO HAS LOST ITS GREATEST CITIZEN

THE WEATHER

TODAY

PUBLIC ALWAYS HAD DEFENDER IN F. G. BONFILS

Publisher Fought Hard For Clean, Honest Government.

Colorado's Foremost Citizen—Frederick G. Bonfils, publisher of THE DENVER POST, died at his home in Denver early Thursday. Mr. Bonfils had been ill one week from an ear infection.

INFLAMMATION OF BRAIN WAS DEATH CAUSE

Mr. Bonfils' Valiant Fight Against Disease Amazes Doctors.

PRESIDENT HOOVER DEEPLY GRIEVED BY F. G. BONFILS' DEATH

Vice President Curtis and Other National Leaders Express Sorrow at Passing of Famous Publisher of THE DENVER POST.

ALL DENVER PRAISES FREDERICK G. BONFILS

FUNERAL SERVICE FOR MR. BONFILS 3 P. M. SATURDAY

The Denver Post mourned the loss of its leader with an "extra" on February 2, 1933.

Courtesy of The Denver Post.

Papa's Girl

GRETCHEN WEBER
Denver Post Artist

F.G. Bonfils didn't have a son, so he had persuaded a nephew, Major Fred W. Walker, to change his name to Bonfils with the idea that he would become his heir. "Maj," as we called him, was *The Post*'s business manager.

At the funeral, prominent Coloradans and visitors from out of state filled the mansion's rooms and a crowd gathered outside. The stocks of local florists were exhausted and the Bonfils' home was filled with floral tributes.

Maj was relegated to sitting on the spiral staircase. Oh, Helen was jealous! She felt he had tried to usurp her role as her father's successor.

DONALD SEAWELL
Helen's Attorney

Helen told me she learned that her father planned to name Major Fred Bonfils his heir and publisher of *The Post*.

She marched into her father's office and told him she knew he had changed his will and she wouldn't have it. He admired her spunk and told her he would name her his successor.

In his will, Bonfils left $50,000 a year to his wife for life. To Helen he left $25,000 a year for life. After Belle Bonfils' death, her annuity would go to Helen, making Helen's payment $75,000 a year.

To May he left $12,000 a year so long as she remained married to Clyde. But if she divorced him or was widowed, her annuity would become $25,000 a year for life. He left $25,000 to Major F.W. Bonfils plus $10,000 "for the education (exclusively and for no other purpose) of his two children." There were bequests of $1,000 to several *Post* employees, including his presumed daughter with

Madge Reynolds, drama editor Betty Craig. Betty, who never married, once explained that she changed her last name from Reynolds to Craig because a numerologist had told her the five-letter name would bring her good luck.

If it was true that Betty was the love child of Bonfils and Mrs. Reynolds, she inherited nothing of her parents' good looks. Nor did the name change bring good luck. She had a face like a little bulldog and one withered arm as the result of a tramway accident. But she did inherit the same slender legs both May and Helen possessed. There was, somehow, always a bond between Betty and Helen.

Bonfils had left the bulk of his estate in a trust to be administered by two banks. As trustees, the banks were obligated to manage the trust according to the wishes of the principal beneficiaries, who were, of course, his wife and Helen. And since Belle was elderly (and suffered from forgetfulness as a result of a series of small strokes), control of the stock was effectively in Helen's hands.

What Bonfils should have realized was that Colorado law entitles a widow to claim half of her late husband's estate, if he doesn't leave her as much. On the advice of her attorney, Belle exercised this widow's option in June of 1933, four months after her husband's death, and broke the will. She claimed as much of *The Post* stock as she was entitled to, which made it available to her heirs instead of the foundation Bonfils had set up.

May was hurt and angry at receiving less than half the annuity Helen was to have. Her husband, Clyde Berryman, had been in Texas, but when he returned, he encouraged her to challenge the will. She filed suit, contending that the provision limiting her benefits to twelve thousand dollars while she was married to Clyde was "contrary to public policy and good morals." Helen agreed—and, more importantly, so did the judge; he ruled that May was entitled to the full $25,000.

ROBERT STOUFFER
Chauffeur

F.G. left minor bequests to relatives and employees at the house. He left me $1,000.

Although I had considered taking one of several jobs that were offered to me after Mr. Bonfils' death, Mrs. Bonfils and Helen asked me to remain with them, as they needed me more than ever. F.G. asked me to look after them several times before his death. So I remained on the job. They told me my work would consist solely of management of the place. It did not take me long to find out that my work would be more confining than it had previously been.

Mrs. B. and Helen told me they would build a home for me and my family on three lots of their property. This, however, never came to pass.

CHAPTER TEN
Miss Helen Comes Out of Papa's Shadow

Helen was forty-three when her father died. By all the reckonings of the day, she was an old maid.

At first, a great dullness clouded her heart and senses. Mama, Helen, and the servants drifted silently around the fifty-room mansion. Papa's presence seemed to linger everywhere.

Then Helen bestirred herself and took over his office at *The Denver Post*. Papa's paper had always been a wondrous place to Helen, with its city room full of shirt-sleeved men bent over upright typewriters, clacking away on their stories. Others, wearing eye shades, sat around the horseshoe-shaped copy desk, checking reporters' stories and writing headlines. Brass spittoons were scattered about the newsroom, and a blue haze of cigar and cigarette smoke hovered overhead. Only two or three women were to be seen. It was a thoroughly masculine profession, an atmosphere Helen considered sheer perfection.

The reporters, almost all young men, came in from the streets and their beats with the latest news, anecdotes and scandals, exuding their insiders' sense of urgency. Rubbing their hands together, they would settle down to their typewriters to pound out their stories before fast-approaching deadlines. Sometimes the city editor ripped sheets of paper from their typewriters as they completed a page and gave them to copy boys to be rushed to the linotype operators. But, often, there were periods of leisurely bonhomie, when reporters lounged around each other's desks, guffawing at stories. They were smart and quizzical and quixotic, and Helen loved their blasé attitude. Frequently, their clothes looked as though they had been slept in, and at times they had.

In a single night, a reporter might witness more drama than the average person sees in a lifetime. And newspapering, Helen learned, is a young man's game. A newsman could barely live on his meager salary, let alone support a wife and family. There was no such thing as a forty-hour week. Reporters might be called in at a moment's notice, at any hour, when all hands were needed to put out an extra, such as when Lindbergh flew the Atlantic, or when a tragedy struck. In a few years, working conditions would change when the Newspaper Guild was formed—to the dismay of Post executives. For a time, management withheld bylines as punishment.

Helen came to know the reporters, the sportswriters, the artists, and the copy editors. She would perch on the desk of the society editor, Harry Lou Gurtler, to exchange tidbits of gossip and news. She was fascinated by Denver's elite, the personages of that rarefied strata which had so successfully held the Bonfils at arms' length ever since she could remember. And now she was in a position to know (in fact, she felt it was imperative that she be informed) of their foibles, their strengths and weaknesses—who was cheating on whom, in business or the bedroom, who wasn't speaking to whom, and so forth. Papa's list of enemies, persons not to be mentioned in *The Post*, was respected and, in time, she added a pariah or two of her own.

HARRY LOU GURTLER
Post Society Editor

Miss Helen would stop around and visit everyone. With those piercing blue eyes, makeup, and blonde hair, she was really an imposing person.

There were eight or ten people never to be mentioned in the society column, and, as I recall, that edict came from her.

She also had an unwritten rule that we never mention her in the society columns. Her father and Mr. Tammen had the same rule in their lifetimes. She was a strong woman, almost zealous in keeping her private life secret. I certainly wouldn't have wanted to cross her.

She could also be very thoughtful. When I married Arnold Gurtler, owner of Elitch's Gardens, Miss Helen sent a limousine and driver to take me to the church and reception knowing my mother couldn't afford it.

Even when you didn't see her, you might be aware of her presence by the scent of Belogia wafting on the air. She sprayed it on pretty generously. One time an advertising salesman, Tex Gressett, stopped by my desk, beaming. "I'm going to smell good all day," he said. "I just passed Miss Helen in the stairwell."

Helen had always felt most at ease with simple folk, so she visited with the men who typed stories on the looming linotype machines in the backshop and learned about their families. She waved to the pressmen, dressed in ink-smudged overalls and wearing hats folded out of newspapers, who supervised the finished editions as they whirred off the big black presses. She was so warmly friendly and genuine in her interest in them that her employes became very fond of her.

She learned that *The Post*'s handsome, white-maned artist, Paul Gregg, always knew the raciest new jokes, and she took to stopping by his desk to hear them and, in time to offer some of her own.

She got to know the advertising salesmen on the first floor, where her cousin, Major F.W. Bonfils, was making do in his "second best" role as business manager.

She always had time for a word with Betty Craig, her presumed half-sister, the amusing young artist Gretchen Weber, and reporter Frances Wayne, who had been there since the century was a pup. They were among the few women in the city room.

To her, everyone was "darling" or "honey," but she was especially close to rakish Al Birch, *The Post*'s longtime publicist who would become director of *The Denver Post* Operas. The operettas were staged each summer in Cheesman Park for thirty-eight years, beginning in 1934, Helen's gift from *The Post* to the people of Denver.

She left the running of the paper to Bill Shepherd—Shep—Bonfils' longtime lieutenant, who had been named publisher. She didn't try to influence the paper's policies. What did she know about politicians or economics? Instead, she staked her claim to realms that held almost no interest for the men of the newspaper—the drama and society columns.

The charming, gracious Anne Sullivan was her secretary, as she had been for Bonfils for a number of years. Anne had made herself even more dear to Mama and Helen when she used her gentle persuasion to convert Papa to Catholicism during his final illness.

Now Helen read the paper from cover to cover as her father had, though without his acute comprehension, she would admit. The new president, Franklin D. Roosevelt, was busy introducing his New Deal. In 1934, Adolf Hitler became the Fuhrer of Germany. But people seemed downright fatuous about the Dionne quintuplets in Canada. Personally, she didn't find babies that interesting.

She was, she discovered, a woman of some prominence. One day the rival *Rocky Mountain News* featured her in its people column. Its readers apparently were intrigued to learn that she was a familiar figure at fashion shows and had acquired one of the finest fur collections in the West and that her height and superb carriage helped her carry off a reputation as one of Denver's best-dressed women. Her favorite hat was a large picture-brimmed chapeau or a poke bonnet, but always with a Lily Dache label. She was said to have "the trimmest ankle in town."

The column noted that she was at St. Philomena's Catholic Church each morning at six o'clock for early Mass with her maid, Fanny, and that she rarely entertained in a grand manner, preferring small get-togethers.

She would have been aware that all this attention must have left May—by now locked in a contentious, loveless marriage—simmering with resentment.

Now that Papa was gone, Helen was free to spend money as she pleased—though years of parsimony had made her prudent in many respects. She was also free to date anyone she wished—if only she knew someone to date. But then she discovered the most precious freedom of all: She was free to pursue an acting career!

The University of Denver Civic Theatre, specifically, beckoned. It was a lively group of theater-struck Denverites—Bohemians, businessmen and socialites alike. And Papa would not have disapproved, because there was not a prostitute in sight.

The Civic warmly welcomed Helen into its ranks. She came to rehearsals in a chauffeur-driven limousine accompanied by Fanny. But everyone called Helen "Bonnie," and she called everyone "honey" (such a handy catch-all when you are as poor at remembering names as Helen was). Her fellow actors said she never tried to hog a scene and that she was free with her compliments and praise. She adored them all. It was sheer magic.

GRETCHEN WEBER
Denver Post Artist

When employees of the *Post* and *News* staged the play Chicago (a version of *The Front Page*) as a benefit for the Denver Press Club, which had been badly hit by the Depression, Helen played the jail matron, a role that called for a frumpy wig and very few lines. The cast fell in love with Helen. She was one of us.

ROBERT STOUFFER
Chauffeur

Shortly after her father's death, Helen became interested in theatricals and began taking parts in the Denver University Civic Theatre plays. Having to accompany her to rehearsals and to presentations, I was asked to take parts in the plays or to do backstage work such as handling properties, prompting, making sound effects, and so forth.

Those plays included *Once in a Lifetime, Rain, Nothing But the Truth, The Little Foxes, Arsenic and Old Lace,* and others.

There was a time when Helen was taking singing lessons and had hopes of becoming a vocalist, until her instructor told her that although she had a strong voice, she would never excel in that line.

CHAPTER ELEVEN
BELLE BONFILS DEPARTS

DR. OSGOOD PHILPOTT
Denver Dermatologist

June 3, 1935.
A little more than two years after F.G. Bonfils death, I arrived at my office to find my receptionist in a state of agitation.

Before I could even set down my black bag, she said, "You have to go to the Bonfils' house immediately."

I was there in ten minutes, and you've never heard such a bedlam of sobbing and wailing. The cook, the chauffeur, the gardener—some ten or fifteen people—were milling about. Helen was there, moaning and grieving and making a commotion, too. It was like a show. And there was Belle Bonfils, lying dead at the bottom of the long circular staircase. She had suffered a heart attack about three-fourths of the way down the stairs. I took out a syringe and gave her an injection in the heart, but it was no use. She was cold and lifeless; there wasn't any pulse or heartbeat.

Just then, in came another doctor. He went up two or three steps and shouted to the wailing people, "Shut up! There never was a Bonfils who wasn't a goddamned fool!"

He was an arrogant German, but he quieted them down.

CHAPTER TWELVE
ESTRANGEMENT

Helen and Mama had grown closer after Papa's death. Too close, May would have thought. Belle, ever more forgetful, had grown quite dependent on Helen for major decisions as well as for the trivia of everyday life. Her estate was valued at an estimated $10 million. She said it was her intent that it should "be divided as nearly equally as possible" between Helen and a trust for May.

May was horrified at Belle's idea of equality when she learned the terms of the will. Helen was to receive her share outright while May's was to be held in trust. She would receive only the income during her lifetime. If May died first, the principal would go to Helen. Helen was also made a gift of the mansion and all of Mama's personal effects.

May was even more infuriated when she learned that all of Mama's holdings in *Denver Post* stock were to be included in the share set off for Helen, who was to continue as Bonfils' successsor at the newspaper. Another vinegary splash on these open wounds was that Helen was named the executor of the will and, also, of the trust to be set up for May's share of the estate.

May sued the next month, charging that Helen had used "undue influence" on Belle to dictate the terms of the will. She said that, at seventy-two years of age, Belle was "so weakened in mind and body" that she lived under Helen's "domination." May also claimed that Helen was "actively hostile" toward her and could not administer the will in a fair and impartial manner.

Two years before, in the compromise settlement of their father's will, Helen had insisted that the court appoint a guardian ad litem to represent "the interest of possible future issue of Helen Bonfils." May, who was fifty-two, said pointedly that Helen was forty-six, unmarried, and quite unlikely to have any children. Helen, who never told her age, was predictably furious in return.

The sisters were both somberly dressed—as the *Rocky Mountain News* noted—when they appeared for the court hearing. The judge ruled that if the case was tried in district court, May would have to offer proof of her charges. Helen could not bear the thought of the publicity—the glaring front page headlines—if they went to trial. Earlier, the *News* had reveled in rehashing all the juicy details of the so-called feud that Frederick Bonfils' will occasioned. A compromise settlement was reached, with Helen and May agreeing to an equal distribution of the Bonfils' fortune, a large part of which was stock in *The Post*. Helen held one more share than May.

That day in court was the last time the sisters communicated with each other, and then it was only through their lawyers and the judge.

From the time May was married in 1904 until Papa's death in 1933, a span of almost thirty years, she and May had remained on good terms. But, increasingly, their relationship had grown strained. When May and Clyde first returned to Denver, they took some delight in renewing their friendly little conspiracies with Helen, and Helen would sometimes meet a beau at their house on Lafayette Street. As Helen grew into her thirties and forties, however, their paths diverged. May must have fretted when she compared their circumstances—Helen lived in the mansion on the hill, basking in Papa's and Mama's affections and enjoying such privileges as a chauffeured limousine, furs, fine fashions, and the attentions of servants, while May made do in her obscure circumstances. Then there were the hurtful slights of the favoritism she saw in her parents' wills and Helen's election as secretary treasurer of *The Post*. Suddenly, Helen had become a public figure, whose generous gifts to numerous institutions were frequently reported, whereas May had become an unmentionable in the newspaper's pages. Oh, it was almost too much to bear! But it would be twenty-five years before May felt empowered enough to unleash her furious resentment.

The passing years—and coping with Clyde's shenanigans—had drained May's once pretty face, leaving a strained expression and down-turned mouth.

But, Helen might have asked, was she responsible for May's misfortune? Was it her fault that May had eloped with a ne'er-do-well drummer who had turned into a drunk to boot?

May was right about one thing: Helen had helped Mama "re-think" her will. It happened in 1933 when Belle and Helen were traveling to New York to meet May. May was upset when they were a day late. Mama, in some confusion, explained that Helen thought they should stop over a day in Kansas City. What Belle didn't tell her eldest daughter was that the First National Bank of Kansas City was co-executor of her will and that she and Helen had re-drafted the document there to Helen's greater advantage.

But, after all, Helen might have reasoned, wasn't she the daughter who had remained single, forsaking the husband and children which most of her contemporaries enjoyed, to abide by Papa's rules and to care for Mama in her somewhat dotty years? And it was Helen—not May—who had stood up to Papa and won his blessing as his successor at *The Post*. Mama understood all that. Why was May so blind to the facts?

CHAPTER THIRTEEN

A BRIDE AT LAST
HELEN, CENTERSTAGE

Helen's success with the Denver Civic Theatre Company gave her the courage to think about something that had previously been unimaginable. Was it possible she could act professionally?

One spring day in 1934, she carefully arranged her now-blondined hair (which she tinted with the help of her maid, Fanny), arrayed herself in a smart navy blue outfit with a little white collar, and set off to audition at Elitch's Theatre. To her stunned delight, the director, Adison Pitt, selected her from among a dozen hopefuls as a member of the theater's professional stock company for the summer season.

She wasn't young, she wasn't gorgeous, but Pitt obviously thought he saw in her the talent of a character actress. When he referred to her as "Miss Barton," Helen corrected him. She was actually Helen Bonfils, she explained. She had used her mother's maiden name to audition because she didn't intend to fail as a Bonfils.

Elitch's was founded in 1890 and had a storied history. The little white wooden playhouse with green trim set in the midst of charming floral gardens in North Denver had once featured Sarah Bernhardt; it had helped launch the Hollywood and Broadway careers of Harold Lloyd, Tyrone Power, Frederic March and his

Papa's Girl

wife, Florence Eldridge; it provided the path to stardom for Edward G. Robinson and Sylvia Sydney. Douglas Fairbanks, a Denver lad, scrubbed its stage for tickets and later acted on its boards. (Robinson was dismissed from the company because he didn't keep up his wardrobe; Florence Eldridge was fired for marrying March. Clark Gable was passed over after an audition and told that he "ought to get his ears fixed.") Grace Kelly joined the stock company in 1951. Helen appeared with her that season.

Helen was forty-three when she made her first appearance on stage that summer in the part of an Italian woman in *Men in White*. She wasn't bad, as it turned out. Much later, her friend Edwin Levy of the drama department of the University of Denver (and sometimes-director of the Denver Civic Theatre) claimed that Helen was one of the most popular actors to appear at the summer theater over

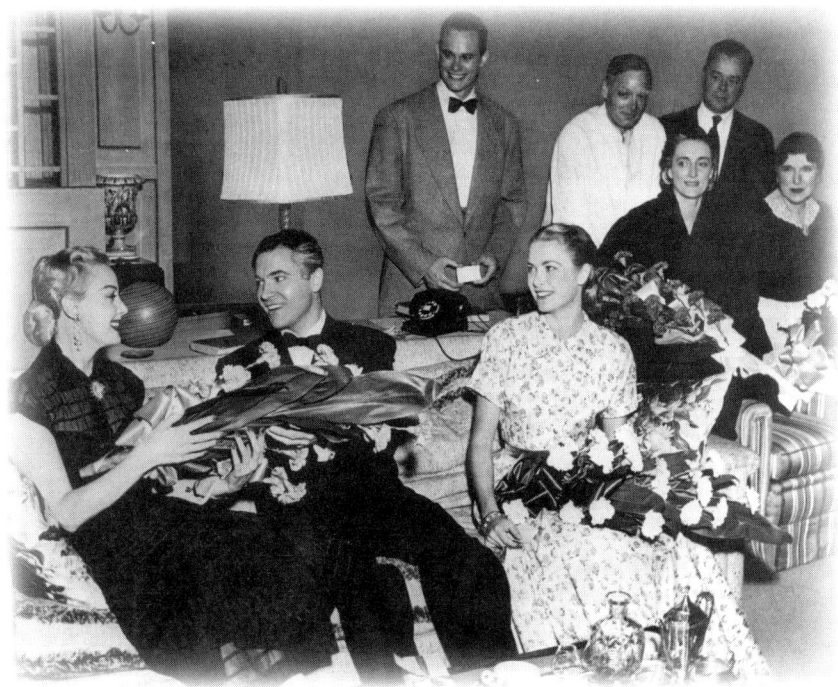

Many future stars appeared at Elitch's Theatre, including a radiant Grace Kelly, shown here (in print dress) in the summer of 1951. At left are Lynn Salsbury and Whitfield Connor. Helen Bonfils, just beginning her acting career in middle age, is at the far right in a maid's costume and dark wig.
Western History Collection, Denver Public Library.

a period of fifteen years. He praised her performances and wrote that she had a "spectacular, versatile flair for bringing vivid characterization" to the secondary parts she played, such as Addie in *The Little Foxes.*

In 1936, Elitch's Theatre hired a new director, a man named George Somnes, who came from Hollywood, where he had been directing films. Helen auditioned for him and, again, she was hired for character roles.

Someone asked Somnes after the audition if he knew who she was, because, once more, she had used the name Helen Barton. When he was told she was Miss Helen Bonfils, the name meant nothing to him. But that would soon change.

One afternoon after a rehearsal, Helen offered him a ride from Elitch's to his hotel. Robert Stouffer, her chauffeur, said later he knew his employer was interested in Somnes because, when he parked the limo across the street from the hotel as was his custom, Helen asked him to drive around the block and let Mr. Somnes off at the main entrance.

Helen would have to acquire a whole new vocabulary to describe George Somnes. He was that different from any man she had ever known. He was amusing, debonair, he had savoir faire. He was also incredibly knowledgeable about the theater and the world. She couldn't help but be bedazzled.

She invited George to dinner at the mansion. They were both a little nervous, she told her good friend, Father John Anderson, some years later. She asked George if he would like a cocktail. He would, indeed. The butler poured a scotch highball for him and served Helen her usual soda with a twist of lime.

Helen was fascinated with George's background—so different from her own, as she learned in the coming months. He had been reared in Florence, Italy, had lived with an aunt in New York, and had traveled abroad extensively.

He had been an actor, and the role of a sophisticated man of the world fit him like one of his well-tailored suits. He had made his stage debut in Mexico City, in a Spanish version of *Lucretia Borgia.* In 1914, the Old Vic Theatre in London suspended tradition temporarily to invite George and several other non-British artists to join its company. He took part in twenty-one Shakespeare productions and won special critical acclaim as King Claudius in *Hamlet*. He traveled further afield as a top sergeant in the 32nd Field Artillery in World War I. After the war, he understudied John Barrymore. To Helen, his classic, chiseled profile was a heart-stopping reminder of Papa.

Before coming to Elitch's, George had directed films in Hollywood for five years, working with the stars Claudette Colbert, Gary Cooper, and George Raft, among others. He was to remain at Elitch's for eighteen years—a record for the summer theater.

He had a merry, ribald streak that suited Helen very well. There was a small difference in their ages—George was a few years younger than she—though, of course, she never let him know that.

And Helen knew she offered her own attractions. True, her once-porcelain complexion was now more heavily powdered and her hair was bleached, but George was not one to be put off by a show of theatricality. And she was wealthy. It pleased her that he was too self-assured to be intimidated by that.

Helen Bonfils and George Somnes made quite a couple. She offered him security, and he offered her entrée into the theater world.
Courtesy of The Denver Post.

There was just one caveat to this romance for which she had waited so long. Marvelous George was gay. She soon realized that there would be no physical relationship. Still, when he proposed, she accepted.

Shortly before the wedding on September 15, 1936, Agnes Tammen, widow of Papa's late partner and a dear friend, hosted a breakfast for Helen. Near the end of the party, she came to the head of the table where Helen sat. She clasped a lovely string of pearls around Helen's throat.

Helen knew the significance of the pearls. For the first dozen years of their partnership, Papa and Mr. Tammen had taken only modest salaries and plowed the profits back into the paper. But one evening, Mr. Tammen came home with a one-hundred-thousand-dollar dividend check which Bonfils had given him that day. He handed it to Agnes, saying, "Here's your string of pearls," knowing how much she yearned for a strand.

"I've changed my mind," Agnes told him. She explained that a group of women had visited her that afternoon to tell her about their plans to start a children's hospital. She said she wanted to give the money to the hospital drive. The Tammens were childless. Later they agreed to make Children's Hospital a beneficiary of their will—and, therefore, a major stockholder in *The Denver Post*.

ROBERT STOUFFER
Chauffeur

I was present at Helen and George's wedding, which Helen told me was merely a business arrangement—she had the money and George had the means for putting her on stage. The wedding was performed at the home of Arnold Gurtler, the owner of Elitch's, by a Catholic priest, although George was an Episcopalian. Helen's friend, Selma, now Mrs. Hubert Kolb, and Arnold Gurtler were the attendants; Fanny and I were also present. Following the wedding, I drove them to New York in a Cadillac that Helen had previously given George. After we got to New York, both Helen and George were insistent that I accompany them on a trip to Bermuda, but I finally convinced them that I'd rather visit my brothers and sisters, whom I'd not seen since I left the East in 1919.

A blizzard which caused much damage to Helen's property in Denver cut short my visit East because, as I had full charge of Helen's home and property, it was up to me to go there and see that the storm damage was cleared up.

On returning from Bermuda, Helen and George rented and eventually purchased a lovely apartment in the River House, New York, which was along the East River and had a remarkable view. They formed a theatrical company, Bonfils and Somnes, and produced several unsuccessful plays. In the summer, George directed plays at Elitch's. I was called on to participate in several of them. Helen was given parts in most of them as well, and also in some of the winter season plays at the Denver Civic Theatre.

CHAPTER FOURTEEN

BROADWAY BECKONS

A year after their marriage, when the summer season at Elitch's was over, Helen and George leased the Little Theatre on New York's Forty-Fourth Street between Broadway and Eighth (now the Helen Hayes) for their theater productions. It was opposite the Shubert and had a seating capacity of between 600 and 700.

Bonfils-Somnes made their Broadway debut with Raymond Van Sickle's *Sun Kissed*, a little comedy with a Los Angeles boarding house locale. Critics treated it like the amusing little trifle it was.

Money, it seemed, could not guarantee a box office hit. Helen appeared (under the stage name Gertrude Barton) in *The Greatest Show on Earth*, a drama with a circus theme. It was not the greatest hit of the season, to put it mildly. *The Brown Danube*, and *Pastoral*, in 1939, didn't fare much better. Nor did *Step This Way*, in 1940. But if you read only *The Denver Post* you might have thought Bonfils-Somnes was a roaring success. Betty Craig, the drama editor, always gave their New York productions glowing reviews—thanks to a little judicious rewriting of the wire services, whose reporters actually attended the performances.

In 1940, however, the couple's luck took a turn for the better when Bonfils-Somnes joined forces with the New York Opera

Company to present *Helen Goes to Troy*. In 1948, they had two successful runs on Broadway with *Make Mine Manhattan* and Moss Hart's *Light Up the Sky*.

If some of their productions weren't wildly successful, George and Helen were, nevertheless, much sought after. The word apparently got around that Bonfils and Somnes had almost unlimited resources. They were in great demand as backers.

New York was every bit as enchanting as Helen had dreamed. Each November the couple moved from the Bonfils mansion in Denver to the gloriously glamorous River House, which George filled with elegant French and Italian antiques and *objets d'art*.

Even during World War II, when so much railway space was commandeered for troops, they could be certain of comfortable accommodations when Robert Stouffer delivered them in the limousine to the train at Denver's Union Station. Helen would be swathed in silver foxes and holding a little dog; George attended in his pinstriped suit and homburg. Helen was aware that they caused considerable head turning, accompanied as they were by their plentiful luggage, and an entourage that now included George's valet, Arthur, and Helen's maid, Fanny. Stouffer would drive the Cadillac on to New York to be at their disposal.

Once in Manhattan, life was an always absorbing round of choosing plays, rehearsing and opening nights, followed by champagne buffets at the River House while they waited for reviews.

Helen had no idea that Denverites visited New York in such droves. They entertained many of them—at tea and cocktails, or dinner in the River House, and they were all stunned by the setting and the view. They also saw a few New York friends for dinner and the theater. On nights when she and George stayed home, they would play piano duets or gin rummy, or perhaps bridge with another couple.

But Denver was never far from Helen's mind. She was in daily telephone contact with *The Post* publisher, Bill Shepherd, and with the current society editor, Georgia Barber, and with drama critic Betty Craig. Even in the midst of New York's glittering theater world, Papa's newspaper was always first in her heart.

CHAPTER FIFTEEN
LADY BOUNTIFUL

After Belle Bonfils' death, Helen found herself a very wealthy heiress, and she embarked on a long spree of giving to Denver and its people. She wanted to erase the ugly stain cast on Papa's name by those who scorned him as a miser, and, too, she basked in the pleasure of giving lavish amounts to Denver and its institutions.

DOROTHY RADER
Bonfils Theatre Boxoffice Manager

Once I had about fifteen minutes of Bonfils Theatre business to discuss with Helen. I arrived at *The Post* on the day of the month when she dispensed checks to the many people she helped. There was a whole line of them outside her office. Helen sat at a desk with her secretary, Anne O'Neil (later Sullivan), and a big checkbook.

As she finished with one visitor—usually a woman—she would call out to the next, "Come right on in, honey." And she would talk to each one. I had to wait a couple of hours to see her.

Papa's Girl

DR. FRANK MCGLONE
Helen's Physician

I was on the board of the Bonfils Foundation. The other members were Dr. Osgood Philpott and Donald Bromfield, a prominent Denver businessman. We seldom met. When we did, Ann Sullivan would give a report on what Helen had done in the way of spending money. She was doing beautiful things but not necessarily in the spirit of the Foundation (which had offered prizes for cures for tuberculosis and cancer). She owned apartment houses, and quite a few people couldn't pay their rent. She would never put them out. What she was doing wouldn't withstand the scrutiny of the IRS. Don resigned from the board over his concerns.

Helen's first major gift was the Holy Ghost Catholic Church, a rose marble structure of graceful Spanish architecture at 1900 California Street in downtown Denver. It was dedicated with proper pomp in 1943 in memory of Belle and Frederick Bonfils.

After that, the requests just kept coming and she was happy to oblige. Helen founded the Belle Bonfils Blood Bank at the Colorado Medical Center (a project dear to the heart of her dermatologist, Dr. Osgood Philpott); contributions to Central City's Opera Association, the Denver Art Museum, the Denver Zoo, the Dumb Friends League, the United Fund, and many others were common. All of the donations came from the Bonfils Foundation, of course.

One of her favorite projects was *The Denver Post* Opera, presented free to the people of Denver on several summer nights each year under the stars in Cheesman Park. Al Birch rewrote the librettos of hits by Sigmund Romberg and Oscar Hammerstein, thereby sparing the newspaper the copyright costs.

This pretty bit of piracy would have pleased Bonfils, but, in later years, Helen actually paid for the rights to produce recent Broadway hits, and for young Broadway stars to appear.

On the days of the performances, hundreds of Denverites would begin arriving in the morning, spreading out their blankets

Opening night at the Bonfils Memorial Theatre, October 14, 1953, was a gala event, calling for gowns and tuxes.
Courtesy of The Denver Post.

and unpacking their picnics, to be assured of seats. As many as 10,000 would be on hand when the mayor and other dignitaries appeared at twilight on opening night to welcome them.

One summer when Helen felt that the Fourteenth Street parade in *Hello Dolly* needed more pizazz than a band and a troupe of horsemen, she arranged for the loan of Bonnie, a young elephant she had given to the Denver Zoo.

In 1971, the thirty-ninth and last year the "opera" was presented, her chauffeur at that time, Joe Farrow, pulled the limousine near the stage on opening night. An ailing and aged Helen wore a fur-trimmed negligee and sat with Father John Anderson in the back seat, eating hot dogs, awaiting the performance. She was no longer able to take her front-row seat.

But of all the philanthropic gifts she dispensed over the years, the most dear to her heart was the Bonfils Memorial Theatre, which she built in 1953 in memory of her parents. It became the new home of the Denver Civic Theatre, where she had had her first experience as an actress back in the forties.

Together, she and Somnes planned the building at East Colfax Avenue and Elizabeth Street. By 1953, Helen was often laid low by phlebitis, but George was at "the Bonfils," as it came to be known, daily, overseeing the design and construction. For the interior, he chose a color scheme of pumpkin and soft blue, shades he believed were the most flattering to Helen.

When it was completed, it was pronounced a jewel box, with its deep-pile carpet, luxuriously upholstered seats, spacious wardrobe rooms and what were said to be the finest dressing rooms in the country. And, of course, it had the very latest in technical theater equipment.

On opening night, October 14, 1953, searchlights scanned the heavens and there were radio microphones and newsreel and television cameras in the lobby as Denverites began arriving in evening gowns, furs and tuxedos to celebrate the inauguration of the city's first new legitimate theater in more than forty years. Telegrams of congratulations from luminaries, including President Eisenhower, were displayed on a bulletin board in the lobby.

Helen loved to dress up for a night on the town.
Courtesy of The Denver Post.

Papa's Girl

The opening production was *Green Grow the Lilacs*, upon which the musical *Oklahoma* was later based. Helen and George stood in the flower-banked lobby to greet the more than five hundred first-nighters. The elaborate programs given to each carried a hand-written dedication by Helen: "I welcome you warmly to the opening night of the Bonfils Memorial Theatre tonight. This playhouse was erected in remembrance of my parents and I hope it will mean to Denver what this city meant to them during their years spent here."

"The Bonfils" went on to have a long and checkered history, and in 2006, after being vacant and shuttered for decades, it was refurbished and reopened as the Tattered Cover bookstore.

CHAPTER SIXTEEN

THE SATURDAY EVENING POST COMES CALLING

In the 1940s, *The Saturday Evening Post* was the most prestigious and popular periodical in the country. But when Mary Ellen Murphy called and said she and her husband Mark would like to write a story about George and Helen for the magazine, Helen of course said no.

Helen was shy and in many ways insecure. That's why she was drawn to acting; she could lose herself in a role and forget who she was.

Mary Ellen was not easily dissuaded. "I don't think you realize what a rarity you are," she might have pointed out. Not only was Helen the owner of a major newspaper (certainly a rarity in that day) but a Broadway actress as well. Helen could have demurred that she wasn't the owner, just majority stockholder. And although she occasionally acted in plays, she wasn't a famous actress by any means.

But Mary Ellen countered that Helen and George were making ripples in New York. And, she could honestly say, "Do you realize any other Broadway producer or actress would do anything—I mean, they would sell their mothers!—to be in *The Saturday Evening Post*? You do know it has the largest circulation of any magazine in the country, don't you?"

George and Helen finally agreed to talk it over with Mary Ellen and Mark Murphy in the River House. The writers were charming and convincing. Disarmed, Helen and George invited them to Denver to visit the mansion and *The Denver Post*. Helen gave them free rein to tour the newspaper and interview its editors. The magazine's photographer, Victor de Palma, shot scenes of Helen at home holding her pet bulldog and poodle in her lap, and took more photos of George and Helen strolling on the sidewalk in front of *The Post* and of the chief lieutenants at work in the city room. The Murphys found Helen's so-called "friends" on their own.

The article appeared in the December 23, 1944, issue, which featured a cover illustration by Norman Rockwell of a Christmas crowd of GIs and civilians in New York's Grand Central Station. Despite the heart-warming wrapping, it was not a pretty present.

"God knows what the late Frederick G. Bonfils, who, with his partner, Harry Tammen, built *The Denver Post* into one of the most raucous and annoying newspapers in the country, would think of his paper and his favorite daughter, if he could see either of them now," the article began.

Helen was stunned at what she was reading. "Bonfils and Tammen ran a hard, greedy sheet; it was often called a blackmailing rag, and both it and the men who ran it could inspire admiration and hatred . . . . The paper makes no local enemies now, though, saving its squeals—which were once roars—for such menaces as the Japanese in internment camps and the Democrats in Washington."

". . . the reading matter beneath the raging headlines is little different from that appearing in any other undistinguished newspaper in any other American city."

Then it was Helen's turn:

"Helen Bonfils would startle her parents somewhat too. She has married a man connected with the stage, has become an actress, lives a good part of the time in New York and gives a lot of Bonfils money away, sometimes without even getting a receipt . . . .

"The town looks upon her with pride and affection. She has gained this respect through effort and a genuine graciousness and charity. As an angel of bounty, she looks like a superannuated chorus girl, having that sort of taste in clothes and a similar manner.

. . . One of the town's games of an evening is guessing her age. The guesses run from forty to sixty." (Helen was fifty-five.)

The article reported that after Helen returned from finishing school, she "had as much social life as the town and her father would allow, which wasn't much. A woman recalled not long ago, 'I never saw her at the Cotillion Ball, the Club Ball, the Charity Ball, the Denver Club or the New Year's Eve party at the country club—the big social events of the year. In the first place, no one liked old man Bonfils; in the second place, he wouldn't have let a boy take Helen to a party if she had been invited; and in the third place, there was her chorus-girl appearance. She was really a sweet girl, and she was as gracious then as she is now, but she did, the Lord knows, dress dramatically.'"

The article rehashed the "unamicable disputes" May and Helen engaged in after Papa's and Mama's deaths, a subject particularly painful for Helen. And to have the family's dirty laundry aired in such a big national publication! The Murphys wrote that Broadway was a little suspicious of Bonfils and Somnes and looked upon them as amateurs in a professional's business: "Helen and George, in the order that people talk of them, work hard both in New York and each summer at Elitch's, where Helen's best parts are considered to have been in *Whiteoaks*, in which she played the 101-year-old matriarch; in *Call it a Day, Morning's at Seven, The Royal Family* and in *Murray Hill*, in which, during the drunk scene, she crawled about on her hands and knees and awed Denver."

The Bonfils mansion was dismissed as a jokey museum piece, with Helen's bedroom described down to her little twin beds.

The Murphys ended their dissection by quoting Helen: "*The Post* is Papa's monument. It is like he was, dynamic, protean and strong, with the strength of a virile man . . . I'll always live in my father's shadow."

"And so will her newspaper," they concluded.

Helen was beyond devastated. Utterly humiliated, when she had assumed she would be put on a pedestal, she never again submitted to an interview with any writer, unless it was a thoroughly trustworthy employee of *The Post*, and then only if her publisher said it was absolutely necessary. Not only had the Murphys trashed her in the great *Saturday Evening Post*, but she had given them license to demean Papa and his paper, two things she held most dear in the world.

Helen had every December 23 issue of the magazine she could get her hands on rounded up and destroyed.

CHAPTER SEVENTEEN
A New Chauffeur

Helen's pleasure in the grand opening of the Bonfils Theatre was only diminished by the pain of phlebitis, which had made it very difficult for her to stand, smiling, greeting people, trying hard not to grimace, for what seemed an eternity.

In 1948, Dr. Philpott had discovered a swelling in one of her legs. He sent her to Dr. Frank McGlone, who diagnosed the problem as phlebitis. Frequently thereafter she suffered from swelling and pain in the leg making it difficult for her to walk.

DR. FRANK MCGLONE
Helen's Physician

One Sunday morning in 1950, I was summoned from a softball game at St. Thomas Seminary, where a group of Denver business and professional men were playing the seminarians. I took a telephone call reporting that Helen was "very sick," and I hurried to her home, still in my dirt-and-sweat-stained clothes. The clot in her vein had worked its way up to the vena cava, the main vein carrying blood back to the lungs before it goes to the heart. There was a big blood clot in the lung, but she didn't want to go to the hospital. The main treatment was to keep the blood from clotting, and I had to keep hot packs on her leg and have regular blood tests. The tests were shuttled from her home to the hospital by limousine. That was one time when it would have been advisable for her to go to the hospital. She was seriously ill for several weeks, but came out of it very well. She improved surprisingly and in several months she was able to go to New York.

Part of the blood clot that went to the lung caused scar tissue so that she didn't have complete lung capacity and that put a strain on her heart. She wasn't always able to go to her office at *The Post* daily, as she had in the past, and she began to receive visitors reclining on the chaise lounge in her boudoir to discuss newspaper and theater business. Sometimes it was necessary for Helen to be carried back and forth from her bedroom to the limousine and to appointments and engagements.

ROBERT STOUFFER
Chauffeur

During the first few years of Helen and George's marriage, George was very agreeable with me, but he soon resented my authority and did everything he could to make things difficult for me. George was an alcoholic who tippled throughout the day and by late evening would sometimes get pretty well lit up—particularly when Helen was not around. I upbraided him on this and on occasion I would try to sober him up before taking him home. He told me that his doctors had warned him that continuation of his drinking would cause his death. But that didn't stop him.

My wife, Anna, died in 1947 after an illness of two years. In 1948, Helen and George Somnes complained that the Bonfils mansion was too great an expense to keep up and too large for their needs. In 1949, they bought the Randolf Morris home, a Mediterranean villa at 707 Washington Street. I spent a good deal of time working with a contractor getting the place livable. There were many defects in the new place—the servants' quarters' roof leaked, plumbing was bad, and heating was inadequate. The driveway, which had been made for a horse and buggy, was much too narrow for our cars. When I called attention to the needed repairs, George would get mad and start to cuss.

Papa's Girl

The Bonfils-Somnes home at 707 Washington Street was in the Italian Renaissance Revival style.

Western History Collection, Denver Public Library.

In February 1950, I took sick with a virus, pneumonia, and was hospitalized. After I left the hospital, my health didn't improve, so, at the doctor's recommendation I had my teeth extracted (all in one sitting) which was a pretty heavy jolt for me.

When I saw I was unable to continue with my work, I had a talk with Helen. She told me there was no provision made for my disability or retirement and suggested that I take a year's vacation without pay. I decided to seek other employment as soon as I was able. During my illness George Somnes talked pretty mean to me—asked if I thought they were running a hospital, and so forth. I realized that so much of my life had been devoted to the Bonfils family that I had neglected my own family; my loyalty of more than thirty years and tasks performed beyond line of duty were unappreciated. Helen even remarked, "If you get hungry, come here and we'll give you something to eat." I was fifty-four when I left the Bonfils-Somnes' employment.

George advertised for a new chauffeur in *The Denver Post*, a blind ad that didn't mention the name of the would-be employer. From several applicants, he selected Mike Davis for an interview.

"What's his experience?" Helen would have asked.

"He's a truck driver," would have been the answer.

And Helen might have been somewhat taken aback. Did she really need a truck driver to haul her up and down stairs? Robert had been such a gentleman, so bright and well-spoken.

Arthur, George's butler, escorted the candidate to Helen's boudoir for an interview. Reclining on her chaise lounge, Helen saw standing before her a young man in his mid-twenties, short, bespectacled, dark and prematurely balding, certainly not particularly prepossessing. As for Michael Edward Davis, it is likely he could barely conceal a double take at the sight of his prospective employer's voluptuous bosom, amply swelling beneath her chiffon peignoir.

Helen would have been entertained by his robust self-confidence and the way he flattered her, to the point that she could overlook his atrocious grammar. As her friend, Haila Stoddard said, she always enjoyed unconventional people—much more than the pale, proper personalities to whom she was most often exposed.

Still, the candidate was of only medium height—several inches shorter than Helen when she was wearing her four-inch heels. Would he be able to carry her down the staircase to the limousine, and back again? Davis would have been very confident about that. And if presented a bulging bicep for her to feel, Helen would no doubt have felt a little thrill. Helen gave George her approval to hire the young man.

Mike's inexperience as a chauffeur, and his excitable temperament, did eventually cause a problem, and George came close to firing him after he wrecked a Cadillac limousine in New York. Instead, George gave him a lecture, and Mike stayed on to prove himself more enterprising than anyone (especially George) had anticipated.

CHAPTER EIGHTEEN

HAILA AND WHIT

In the summer of 1953, the very pretty, vivacious actress Haila Stoddard joined Elitch's company. Haila was a rising star on Broadway, and in Denver she sparkled brightly. She fell in love with her leading man, Whitfield Connor, and their love scenes fairly sizzled on stage that summer.

Helen was enchanted by Haila's amusing, beguiling personality and her heady theatrical experience (roles in Noel Coward and George Kaufman-Moss Hart plays, etc.), but little did she dream when they began sharing a dressing room that their girl talk would eventually lead to a partnership and the smash Broadway hit Helen had so long coveted.

Out of their association would also grow a warm and rewarding friendship with Whit, who would become one of the linchpins of Helen's life.

Haila and Whit were married to others when they met at Elitch's; after several years they were able to sort things out, divorce their mates, and enter into an enduring marriage.

Vivacious actress Haila Stoddard became Helen's partner in theatrical ventures, and a dear friend.
Courtesy of The Denver Post.

HAILA STODDARD
Actress, Friend

George Somnes had talked to me for several years about coming to Elitch's for the summer season as leading lady, but I was never able to because I was in three plays that ran for a total of ten years.

At last, in the early fifties, I was able to accept. George said, "Oh, I'm so glad! We have the handsomest man in the world to be leading man. He's coming from California, where he's been in a film. And Helen Bonfils will be in the company as well."

And who might she be, I wondered. I would soon find out.

Somnes and the Gurtlers (Arnold and his sons, Jack and Arnold Jr., the owners of the theater) used to come to New York to cast the stock company, which was usually composed of eleven members: the leading man, leading woman, second man, second woman, and some of the character parts. Shortly before the season was to begin, the company would take a train to Denver and arrive to a great big welcome at Union Station. It was absolutely marvelous, and very close to the end of that theater stock company era.

I got there a day before Whit. The following afternoon, I was standing outside the theater when I saw a little white Volkswagen bug drive up. I thought, "That's the most amusing auto," and out stepped Whit, who was an extremely handsome man, wearing black leather boots and riding breeches. He looked so dashing. We got on splendidly from the moment we introduced ourselves, and when I got to know Helen, we became very good friends also.

Helen and I used to talk in the dressing room before and after the show. She was very puzzled to learn that I was not enamored of acting. She had dreamed of becoming—yearned to be—an actress. But her father really equated actresses with whores. I think one reason she had such a highly developed sense of the devious was that she did pretty much what she wanted to and Papa didn't know what she was up to.

May defied her father and Helen outwitted him. She would tell me how she would slip out her bedroom window to see a young man, a poet. I think perhaps he was a homosexual? Helen was very naïve about those things.

I told her, "I love the theater; I would never have done anything else." But I said acting had lost some of its charm for me because of the tedium of the long runs, eight performances a week for years and years. I said I would like to go on and be part of the production. I'd like to put the pieces together. I had always liked the rehearsals best.

Helen said, "Well, I'll tell you what; if you ever do anything like that, I don't want you to be involved with anyone else. Would you bring it to me?"

I think Helen and George missed the boat in New York because of a lack of experience on both their parts. George's experience as a director in Hollywood and at Elitch's didn't prepare him for New York's tough, slick standards.

George was very ambitious, and I don't think he ever achieved quite what he wanted. He had a big problem with alcohol and that stopped him as much as anything. To come to New York with a lot of money and be at the mercy of people and not discerning enough—well, we all need sharpening and honing.

In New York, Helen was regarded as Mrs. Moneybags, and she sensed that and resented it.

"I know I'm nobody in New York," she once said to me. "But I really *am* someone in Denver."

Several years after our dressing-room talk I was in New York. Whit had gone back to California. Ours had developed into a great love, but we were both attached. I was working on a daily TV show—I was on The Secret Storm for eighteen years as the original Aunt Pauline—and I was always doing a play at night.

I have enormous energy; I love to work. I would wake up early each morning and I'd have no one to talk to because I was in the theater, and no one else I knew was an early riser. So I invented characters and let them talk to me and I'd talk to them.

I had always loved James Thurber, and I thought, "I can see a way to put this on the stage," and I conceived the idea of *The Thurber Carnival*. When I showed it to Whit, he said, "This works for me. Why don't you show it to Thurber?" This was 1958.

I called Elliott Nugent, with whom I had worked on *The Male Animal*, because I knew he knew Thurber. He said, "Come on up." So I went right away to his apartment. He sat me down at the bar and took the script away. I felt like a father awaiting a birth. When he came back in about an hour, he said, "I think you've got something." I asked if he would call Thurber and he said he would.

Thurber was on the phone when I got home. I went to the Algonquin Hotel to meet him and his wife, Helen. Thurber was blind, of course, so I read the manuscript to him. He said, "I never thought these pictures could come off the page. Yes, you can have the rights." I went to the lobby of the hotel and called Helen. "I have something to tell you," I said. "You once told me if I had something, you wanted to hear it." I went over to her apartment at the River House and for the second time that day I read the script.

I said, "Today I got the rights from Thurber," and she said, "Today you also got the money. Go right ahead, dear."

CHAPTER NINETEEN
A NEW PUBLISHER

The hated *Saturday Evening Post* article kept replaying itself in Helen's head. The Murphys had so stingingly dismissed Papa's paper—now Helen's paper. They had quoted *The Post*'s managing editor, Shep, as saying "a good paper is one that is successful." They scoffed that "by his standards *The Post* is wonderful, making, as it does, more than one million dollars a year." They wrote that the average wage was low, compared with salaries at many major newspapers. (Reporters' salaries ranged from thirty to fifty dollars a week, Helen learned).

But painful as the article was for Helen, because of it she found herself thinking much more intensely about *The Post* as a business than she had in the past. She realized that her daily calls to Shep and the society and drama editors were not enough to keep her fully informed.

Since the newspaper was very profitable, Helen had assumed it was wonderful. The pink front page with its blood-red headlines which she had loved since childhood still looked exciting. How was she to know its content was considered anemic? And the answer was, she should have known; as principal shareholder, it was her business.

And now some of Agnes Tammen's fretting about Shep's obsessive conservatism—his constant damning of the Democrats and Roosevelt's New Deal—began to register with Helen. When she asked a few close associates their opinions—friends like Anne O'Neill, once Papa's private secretary and now Helen's, and her attorney, E. Ray Campbell—they admitted they, too, were put off by *The Post*'s tone.

Shep saw the handwriting on the wall. Late in 1945, almost a year after the magazine article, he was a rather dotty seventy-one years old; thirty-eight of them had been spent working for F.G.'s newspaper. Now World War II was over and the newsprint shortage that had curtailed *The Post*'s growth would be eased. Machines and the metal for setting type would be available, Helen was told. New challenges were just ahead.

Shep, Helen knew, sensed the coolness of the board members; she could see the puzzlement on his face when her customary warm embraces were swift and half-hearted. He offered his resignation.

Ray Campbell was immensely relieved by Shep's decision. Ray, a courtly, discreet North Carolinian who had come to Denver seeking a health cure after he was gassed in World War I, had been Agnes Tammen's personal attorney. As principal trustee of her estate, he was named vice president of *The Post* when she died in July 1942.

Helen turned to Ray to lead a search for a new publisher. The new publisher should be someone under fifty so he could serve *The Post* for the next twenty years. He should have a proven record of successful editorship. And he should be a westerner.

Ray especially liked what he learned about Edwin Palmer Hoyt, editor of the *Portland Oregonian*. *The Oregonian*, Campbell told Helen, was the leading newspaper in that state, with an average daily circulation of 177,327, and a Sunday circulation of 230,071, somewhat smaller than *The Post*'s then 187,801 daily and 306,664 Sundays. Its founder and owner had died around 1930, leaving the stock to his wife and children, and the paper was rapidly going downhill when Hoyt was made managing editor in 1933. He was credited with putting the paper back on its feet. During the war, he agreed to go to Washington as one of the top men in the Office of War Information for six months. After completing his term to some acclaim, he went back to his paper. The fact that the *Oregonian* was family-owned might limit his opportunities there and make *The Post* more attractive to him, Ray thought.

Papa's Girl

Hoyt came for an interview and charmed Helen, Campbell, and the board, as he later did most of Denver, with his quick grasp of *The Post*'s situation, jokes, hearty laugh, and rumbling bass voice. His walk was like the rolling gait of a sailor and his large hands reached out to offer a hearty shake to everyone he met. He was soon "Ep" (short for E. Palmer) to everyone. A contract for five years was drawn, beginning February 20, 1946, that provided for a salary of $40,000 the first year with $5,000 increases each year until he would be paid $60,000. He was forty-eight years old.

Ep had several conditions. He had heard *The Post* had a blacklist (Campbell and Helen denied it), and said it must go. He wanted to institute an editorial page; to modernize the creaky, out-of-date equipment; and to get rid of the paper's sensational makeup. Helen and her officers agreed to everything.

In a few years, Hoyt had upgraded *The Post* to a top-notch newspaper, rated as one of the best in the country. Its prestige was a tremendous satisfaction for Helen.

Before he came, the extent of a reporter's expense account might have been a tram car token for a trip to suburban Littleton, Helen learned. Now Hoyt was sending Leverett Chapin to England

Helen with young Denver Police Band members Roderick Folsom, center, and Gerald Garland at the opening of the new Denver Post building on California Street in May 1950.
Courtesy of The Denver Post.

to report on its program of socialized medicine. Richard Dudman followed a group of Europeans trying to reach Palestine. Palmer Hoyt Jr. was sent to report on the new hotbeds of communism, Korea and China. Robert W. "Red" Fenwick was named to cover the "Rocky Mountain Empire," a thirteen-state area to which Ep had laid claim. Reporters were traveling hither and yon—more jaunting than Helen could keep track of.

Ep soon brought the pay scale for all employees up to levels comparable with those of other metropolitan papers. He speeded up plans for a multimillion-dollar, super-modern plant. All this came at considerable cost, of course, and the board of Children's Hospital, Agnes Tammen's distant relatives, who were minority stockholders, and May Bonfils, all began to question their reduced dividends.

In his early years with *The Post*, Hoyt drank heavily. At one party attended by Denver's elite, Helen was nonplussed to see him nibbling on the ankle of an attractive socialite. She couldn't help comparing this garrulous drinker with Papa, who was not only abstemious but who abhorred any show of drink. She made her feelings known and Ep quit drinking altogether.

Helen sensed that Ep had—as she had said of Papa—the strength of a virile man. This virility would lead to problems.

In June 1949, Ep was sued for divorce by his wife of twenty-seven years, Cecile. Brownie, as most of her new friends called her, had been his college sweetheart and was the mother of their two grown sons. Brownie had resented having to leave Portland for Denver and was having her own problems with the bottle.

Soon after the divorce suit was filed, a scandal erupted. Sometime earlier, Hoyt had sent his outdoor editor, Wally Taber, an attractive blonde fellow, to Africa to write about two prominent Denver businessmen on their big game safari. He returned to find that his wife was having an affair with Ep and wished to marry him.

Despite Brownie's tippling, Helen had been quite fond of her. She had an irreverent, some said abrasive, earthy sense of humor. The new Mrs. Hoyt-to-be, Helen May, was a vivacious brunette of Rubenesque charms who was only thirty to Ep's fifty-two years. Helen took a dim view of her and the whole situation. Nevertheless, the couple was married November 7, 1950.

In time, it got back to Helen that Hoyt had said he could sweet talk her into anything. She was hurt and deeply offended. She still respected him as a publisher, but her feelings toward him, inevitably, changed.

HELEN MAY HOYT
Palmer Hoyt's Wife

Miss Helen didn't like women or wives. She was diffident; she endured me. It hurt me because I had admired her since I was a little girl and used to go out to matinees at Elitch's to see her in all those fifteen-minute parts.

I felt she was trying to drive a wedge between Palmer and me. When we finally managed to get away to Hawaii for a vacation in 1956, George Somnes died and she called asking Palmer to return to be a pallbearer.

Denver Post editor Palmer Hoyt and his much younger bride, Helen May, cut their wedding cake in May 1955. *Courtesy of* The Denver Post.

She called him every day on the phone, no matter where we were. Palmer said they were talking about *The Post*, but it seemed to me they spent a lot of their time telling each other risque stories. Palmer was an incredibly sexy man, and I sometimes wondered if she had designs on him.

I would often go to New York with Palmer for the national meetings of the Editors & Publishers or the Associated Press. On our only free night we would visit George and Helen at their apartment on Riverside Drive, and then Helen usually insisted on taking us to the circus at Madison Square Garden. I mean, I didn't get to see a Broadway play or anything of interest to me. I thought she and George seemed bored with each other.

Miss Helen had some properties around Denver that were little more than tenements. I went to see a dressmaker who lived in one of them on East Colfax Avenue. Believe me, you took your life in your hands when you went up the stairs to her apartment, they were so rotten.

The postwar years not only brought Palmer Hoyt to *The Post* but an influx of male reporters, returning from their service in the armed forces or attracted by *The Post*'s newly enhanced reputation. Women had taken many of their slots while they were away, but now the city room was once more filled with the laughter and bass rumble of men's voices. Some of the women remained; others rejoined husbands or sweethearts back from service.

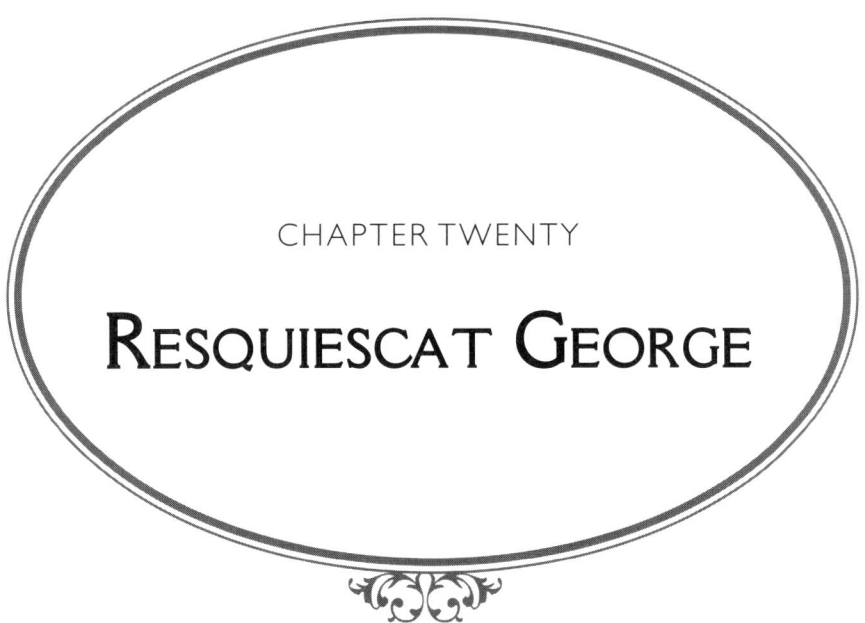

CHAPTER TWENTY
RESQUIESCAT GEORGE

DR. OSGOOD PHILPOTT
Denver Dermatologist

When George Somnes first came to Denver, I asked him if he would like to be a member of the Cactus Club, a rather exclusive club of men who were interested in literature and the arts. He came quite often. I thought he was quite pompous; I thought he boasted a hell of a lot.

He was a snappy dresser. George Somnes was the first man in Denver to wear a jacket, a sports coat, that was different from his trousers.

FRANK RICKETSON
Theater Owner, Self-made Millionaire

Helen was a remarkable woman. I had known her since I was a sports writer at *The Denver Post*, before I got into the movie theater business with Bank Night during the Depression.

Her great love was George Somnes. I remember being in New York on a hot night in the summertime; I had left the Sherry

Netherland to get a little fresh air, and who should I run into on Fifth Avenue but Helen and George, walking along, holding hands.

She was a strong woman, very much opposed to liquor, although she served it at parties.

One time I took George on a hunting trip to Lander, Wyoming, the One Shot Antelope Hunt. It was an annual event for a number of Denver men, and sometimes I would invite a celebrity who was in town, like the tenor Lauritz Melchior. I would get a plane from Bob Six (president of Continental Airlines) to fly us to Wyoming.

I always tried to get about half guys who didn't hunt, like Mayor Quigg Newton. When George joined us, he had on suede shoes and a nice brown suit. He didn't participate in the hunting; in fact, he didn't like the smell of antelope meat. These men who didn't hunt got very comfortable and had a car with good food and lots to drink. George got under a shade tree and drank scotch.

That night I delivered him home, rang the doorbell, and deposited him on the doorstep. The next time I saw Helen she said, "What did you do to poor George? Did he eat some of the antelope? He was sick for three days; he didn't get out of bed."

Helen was quite naive in some ways.

I approached her on many things, for charitable gifts. She always gave freely and never asked me to give but for one cause, the Dumb Friends League. She said, "Rick, you've just got to give."

When the stockyards were holding a drive for a new stadium, they gave me Helen's card. The last thing Helen was interested in was the stockyards, so I hit upon the idea of an educational hall, and told her how it would be a place for kids where they could see rabbits, pheasants, barnyard chickens, lambs, goats, llamas, turkeys. She liked that, and she gave the first amount. That's now the most popular thing at the Stock Show.

I really got to know her through Central City. She arranged for several New York theater hits to play in the old opera house after the summer opera season. She gave $10,000 to sponsor an original play, and I gave another $10,000. (The play, *And Perhaps Happiness*, by Thomas Hornsby Ferril, once a *Denver Post* reporter, was presented in 1958.)

Papa's Girl

DR. FRANK MCGLONE
Helen's Physician

Sometime in 1954, Helen called me from New York saying George was very ill. I flew back, and it was the first time I detected signs of a liver disease. George did drink, but it didn't affect his behavior, only his health.

They came back to Denver and, in time, George was bedfast. Helen had a large bedroom on the second floor, and he had a smaller one on the same floor.

When George died at home early in 1956, Olinger's (a Denver mortuary) had to embalm the body in the bathtub. Helen said her father and mother didn't leave home until they went to the cemetery. Vanderbur (Francis Vanderbur, owner of the mortuary) was aware of that and he was prepared; he came to the house with a crew.

The Post was very important to Helen. When George was dying, she warned me: "When he dies, don't notify anyone until after 10 p.m. so *The Post* will be the first to have the story." (*The News*, a morning paper, wouldn't be able to get a story on the presses in time. *The Post*, an afternoon paper, would get the first headlines.)

PAT COLLINS SMEDLEY
Denver Post Society Editor

Gretchen Weber and I got Christmas presents from Miss Helen—perfume—but they came not from her but from George, who was a darling, darling man. When my husband and I were in New York, she entertained us, usually at the River House. She always started out asking if we wanted tea and George would say, "Helen, you know they want a drink!"

She was very devoted to him and broken-hearted when he died. I think that was one of the hardest things that happened to her.

GRETCHEN WEBER
Denver Post Artist, Fashion Editor

When I became fashion editor of *The Post* I would go to New York for the fall and spring fashion showings, and Helen and George always entertained me.

One time George met me at the door of the River House apartment and he goosed me. In front! I was so mad! And Helen just said, "Oh, George!"

We had dinner at a very long table that would seat about a hundred people. After a while, I said, "Why don't we all move closer together so we can talk?" So we did.

HAILA STODDARD
Actress, Friend

George was a very sophisticated person. He was elegant; he was fun. He dressed flamboyantly, wearing a flowered vest with a striped shirt, for instance. He gave Helen culture. He gave her a certain amount of class, a sort of entree she wouldn't have had otherwise.

I think when George died she felt very guilty. He had been ill a long time, and I think the business with Mike began while he was ill. I know there was a great sexual drive, and that's how Mike got what he did from Helen.

I always thought, with George, it was more of a business arrangement than a marriage.

SHEILA BISENIUS
Helen's Godchild

My mother, Anne, was secretary to F.G. from 1920 until he died in 1933, and then she became Helen's secretary. My earliest memories of Helen are of a lady in a big hat, and I always had to be good when she was around. She didn't like kids much. She liked me when I was a teenager. She'd take me around New York; we'd go to Lily Dache's for hats.

I remember seeing Helen appear with George in the center ring with the Barnum and Bailey Circus in Madison Square Garden in a fancy carriage. She wore a Victorian dress with a big hat and carried a parasol.

George was charming, elegant, affable, delightful—and probably gay.

CHAPTER TWENTY-ONE
MAY REBELS

Things had been looking up for May Bonfils. In 1937, after both her parents' estates were settled, she was on her way to becoming a millionairess—quite a distinction in Denver in those Depression years.

She began construction on Belmar, a mansion of white Carrara marble set on 250 acres in rural Jefferson County on the outskirts of Denver. The home was a replica of the Petite Trianon, the retreat Louis XVI built for Marie Antoinette at Versailles. "Belmar" was a combination of Belle and Mary, the name with which May was christened. J.J.B. Benedict, one of Denver's most distinguished architects, designed the twenty-two room mansion.

Uncle Charlie, F.G's brother, who had once lived with the Bonfils family, now made his home with May, and Helen was indebted to him for details on the grandiosity of her sister's new lifestyle.

A high hedge of Russian olive trees surrounded the property, assuring May's privacy. Behind the hedge, fifty European white fallow deer nibbled the grass in the deer park, another reminder of Versailles. The life-size marble sculptures lining the mall leading to the mansion were copies of European masterpieces and included statues of Diana, Cupid, and Psyche.

Belmar: May Bonfils used her inheritance to build a replica of the Petite Trianon at Versailles on hundreds of acres in the Lakewood countryside. Years later, after May's death, it was torn down.
Western History Collecton, Denver Public Library.

Lily ponds dotted the landscaped gardens, and white swans glided across an azure blue natural lake which covered some fifty acres. At the entrance to the home was a large fountain centered with a statue of Venus by the noted sculptor Canova. (The fountain now graces Hungarian Freedom Park at Speer Boulevard and Emerson Street in Denver.)

Inside the mansion, the Napoleonic crest was embroidered, engraved or carved on any object that lent itself to such branding. (Papa had been proud of the fact that his grandfather was said to have played with the future consul of France when both were boys on the island of Corsica.)

All this May surveyed in lonely splendor. In 1943, ten years after Papa's death, she had legally rid herself of Clyde Berryman in a Reno divorce. She had not lived with him for almost a decade. Throughout their marriage, he worked off and on as a salesman for various concerns. May complained to friends that she even had to give her husband car fare. In the end Bonfils was right; Clyde had intended for his father-in-law to support him.

"I married the first man who came along," May admitted to friends.

Rocky Mountain News columnist Gene Amole once described Clyde as "a cigar-chewing, fancy dressing, sporting type who hung around Burt Davis' Cigar Store" in downtown Denver.

Helen and Belle had heard rumors of his roisterings and drinking and of his foul rages for years. Just five months after Papa's death, on the night of June 16, 1933, his boorish behavior was spread before all Denver in front page headlines in the *Rocky Mountain News*. May had called the police to their home on Lafayette Street and Clyde was jailed on charges of drunkenness and disturbance.

May went to the police station and, unfortunately for her, someone tipped off the *News*. She was pictured on the front page of the newspaper the next morning, being escorted down a corridor of the police building by Chief August Hannebuth. Helen was mortified at seeing the Bonfils name dragged through the mud, and it was undoubtedly even more painful for May.

In a three-column photo, May's blonde hair was mostly confined by a close-fitting cloche hat that matched her stylish dark coat and dress. High-heeled pumps set off her slender legs. A smaller inset photo of Clyde showed a man with fair hair combed back from a high forehead. The features in his long face were undistinguished except for a startled look in his light eyes—probably from having the photographer's flash explode in his face.

According to the story that accompanied the photo, May was ushered into the office of Chief Hannebuth, where she pleaded with him to "take the guns out of my house. Either he will die or I will."

Chief Hannebuth countered, "You are the master of your house."

"I am not the master of my home," May replied. "For many years I have stood for this. Something must be done about it. I am afraid of him."

Papa's Girl
ROBERT STOUFFER
Chauffeur

Around 1934, May became acquainted with a young chap who was attending Regis College with the intentions of entering the priesthood. During Clyde's absence in Texas oil fields, May brought the boy into her home. When Clyde returned and found the boy living there he raised a rumpus during which police were called and a *News* photographer took a picture of May ordering Clyde from the premises with a revolver, and of police arresting him.

Then Clyde started a suit claiming that Belle Bonfils and Helen had caused the break-up between him and May. I was called upon to give a deposition and convinced attorneys that Mrs. Bonfils and Helen were not at fault. On the strength of this, Clyde's suit for $750,000 was dismissed. Clyde was surely mad at me and threatened to cut my heart out the next time we met.

May left Clyde soon after the police were called to her home a second time. For a while she paid him $150 a month to stay out of Colorado, according to newspaper accounts. When he returned to the state, May moved to Reno, established residence, and obtained a divorce. In 1947 she sought and received a second divorce decree in Denver to make doubly sure she was rid of her husband. Her pride and, perhaps, her Catholic faith had kept her in the marriage thirty-nine years.

At Belmar, she lived mostly in isolated splendor. Its multiple rooms included a magnificent small chapel built off the foyer where she could pray, meditate, and attend daily Mass conducted by the brown-robed Benedictine priests from St. Elizabeth's Catholic Church in Denver. For the Benedictine monks, she had built a monastery attached to their church in downtown Denver.

Papa's Girl

ATWILL GILMAN
Helen's Friend

Among the few parties May attended were those given by Mrs. J. Kernan Weckbaugh, the doyenne of a wealthy pioneer Catholic family. What people noticed most when May made an appearance was that she was literally loaded with jewels. When I saw her, she had bracelets, set with precious stones, from each wrist to almost the elbows.

The few visitors she had at Belmar included Harry Winston, the New York jeweler. Her purchases included two of the world's major diamonds, the seventy-carat Indian "Idol's Eye" (she was said to have paid upwards of seven hundred thousand for it), and the thirty-nine-carat Venezuelan stone, "The Liberator." Her "Star of India" emerald and diamond necklace was formerly owned by the Maharaja of Indore.

When Winston called my mother-in-law, Marjorie McIntosh Buell, to report that he was coming to Denver, she said she didn't think it would be worth his while to visit Denver on her account.

"My dear," he reassured her, "my best customer in the U.S. lives in your city." That was May Bonfils.

May had a little dog she loved. She would have the chauffeur drive them to the Lewis Drug Store on West Colfax Avenue almost every night. She would order a cherry limeade for herself and an ice cream cone for the chauffeur to take to the dog in the Rolls Royce.

May liked to browse behind the drug store counters, looking at the lipsticks, rouges, creams, and other cosmetics. Like Helen, she dressed up for the simplest outing, and the drugstore employees were fascinated by her fabulous hats, the most spectacular of which she'd had created for her trip to London for the coronation of Queen Elizabeth in 1953.

MARY MCGLONE
Denver Socialite

My husband, Bill, and I tempted May up to Central City to see a play in the Opera House. We were sitting at the bar of the Teller House next door when a Denver man reeled into the room, much the worse for drink.

When he saw May, he cried, "Helen!" May picked up her handbag and fled into the night with Bill and me following. There was quite a resemblance between the two sisters, particularly for one in his cups, I dare say.

ROBERT WELSH
Antique Dealer, Friend

When Belmar required some redecorating, Fay Curran, a friend of May's, suggested Ed Stanton. Ed had come from modest beginnings in North Denver and started his career as an interior designer at the old Daniels & Fisher's store, where he had a following among Denver's social set. In time, he won quite a national reputation; his commissions included work on the restoration—and almost complete rebuilding—of the White House during Truman's presidency. He was also chosen to work on lobbies and public rooms of the Fairmount Hotel in San Francisco, the Broadmoor at Colorado Springs and the Brown Palace Hotel in Denver.

He and May first met through their mutual interest in the old mining town of Central City, where she set up a memorial fund to take care of the garden between the Teller House and the Opera House.

Ed was a striking man, tall and handsome with black eyebrows that flanged out over his dark eyes. May fell in love and she proposed to him. She told him she wanted someone to help take care of Belmar and to ensure that it would be her home until her death.

If he would fulfill those requirements, she said, she would give him one million dollars when they married and the house and its acreage when she died. Ed accepted, and they were married in April 1956 in Presentation Catholic Church. May was seventy-three and Ed forty-six.

Helen would have learned of May's upcoming marriage from a story in *Cervi's Journal* several days before the wedding.

The account was illuminating on several counts. It reported that May was "one of the wealthiest women in the West, her fortune

Edwin Stanton, May Bonfils' second husband. Shown here with Mrs. Spencer Penrose in Central City in 1954.
Western History Collection, Denver Public Library.

being estimated at between fifteen and twenty million at least." In addition to being "eighteen-to-twenty-percent owner" of *The Post*, the *Journal* said, "she has made a sizable fortune in Denver real estate and in the stock market with the aid and guidance of her attorney, Edgar McComb."

The story explained that the sisters had been estranged for twenty years, adding that while Helen was the subject of many stories in both her own newspaper and others, May "has not been granted the privilege of seeing her name in print in her own newspaper even when she has figured in legitimate news.

"Palmer Hoyt, publisher of *The Denver Post*, denies that May Bonfils is blacklisted, but the fact remains that she has been foreclosed from personal publicity in the paper's columns," the story asserted.

Helen commented to Palmer Hoyt, "He's just marrying her for her money."

In the past, May had complained that her doings went unreported in *The Post*; now Helen saw to it that her sister's remarriage got full coverage. Her society editor, Pat Collins, was assigned to write the account of this romantic news, a touchy assignment.

Collins remembers that Miss Helen asked her to read her story to her over the phone before it went to press. "She wanted to be sure the date of her first marriage was mentioned," Collins said. This was information that was usually tactfully omitted from stories about second marriages.

(Actually, the *Journal's* story had also mentioned that May's previous marriage "performed outside the church of her faith, ended in a divorce from Clyde Berryman and was the subject of a not uncommon dispensation.")

May was already angry at Helen and Hoyt because the paper had carried stories about her two divorces from Clyde. And now she could add another grievance to her considerable store.

May Bonfils married Ed Stanton when she was 73 and he was 46.
Courtesy of The Denver Post.

Papa's Girl

ROBERT WELSH
Antique Dealer, Friend

May was spoiled and selfish and terribly jealous of her younger husband, but he was very, very fond of her. They spent almost half their time in Europe, accompanied by nurses. They were remarried in the Vatican on one of their tours and received the blessing of Pope John XXIII. Since May's first marriage was a civil one, it didn't count in the eyes of the church.

They collected art and furnishings for Belmar on their travels, and the mansion's great rooms were often lighted with chandeliers and candelabras when they entertained friends at small dinners or dined together in state. A valuable portrait of Madame Du Barry by Hyacinthe Rigaud hung in the walnut paneled dining room where May presided at the table.

On special occasions, May would have an armored car bring her a jeweled necklace, earrings, and bracelets from the downtown bank vault. She liked to drape the Idol's Eye necklace or a magnificent emerald and diamond neckpiece around the neck of her poodle.

"Isn't she pretty?" she would cry, and the dog would race up and down the stairs in excitement. Then May would lean over the bannister and call to the servants downstairs, "Don't let that dog out!"

Belmar's walls were hung with valuable tapestries and paintings. The giant table and cabinet in the library were originals from the Versailles Palace, fashioned by the famous Charles Antoine Boulle. Of course, the Napoleonic crest appeared on linens and plaques throughout the mansion, in recognition of Papa's reminiscences of his relationship to "the Little Emperor."

In the grand salon of the mansion, where the panels of pink silk damask were framed in gold, there was a treasure trove of items from Holyrood Palace in Edinburgh and St. James's Palace in London, including a carved gold chair bearing the crest of Victoria Regina, in which Queen Victoria had sat.

May was once asked why there wasn't a twentieth century piece in Belmar. "The twentieth century never existed," she dismissed the period.

Her husband Ed called her "the last of the Victorians."

HELEN BLACK
Co-Founder, Denver Symphony Orchestra

May used to come to the University of Denver Theatre openings in a dingy satin gown, bracelets going from wrist to elbow. Her jewelry looked more grungy than brilliant. On occasion, I would be invited to the Petite Trianon for lunch. That marble home was full of art objects, but dirty.

Ed Stanton earned every cent he got. He cleaned up the house, he cleaned up May and he took her to Europe.

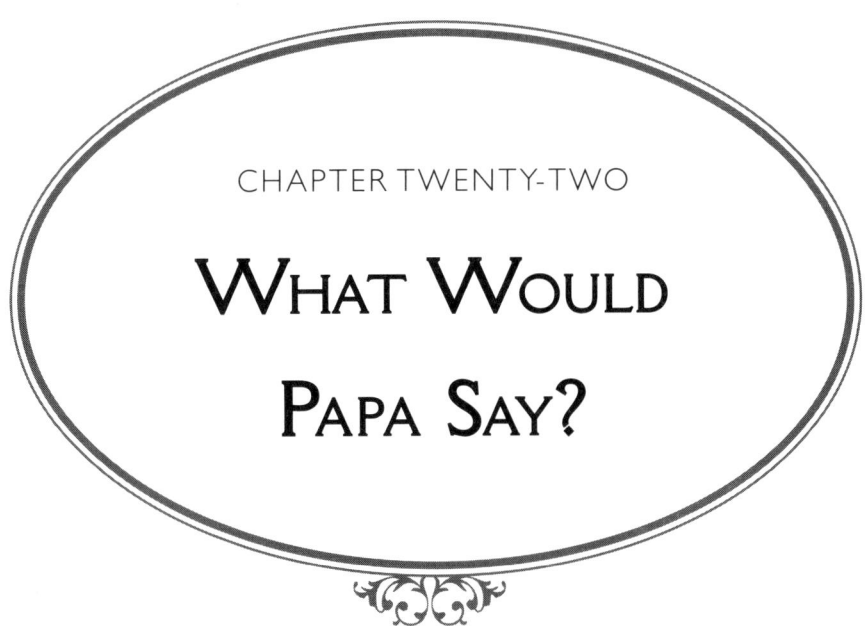

CHAPTER TWENTY-TWO

WHAT WOULD PAPA SAY?

April 2, 1959.
After the judge had pronounced Helen Bonfils and Mike Davis man and wife, he said to Mike, "You may now kiss the bride." Helen bent her knees slightly, because even though Mike was wearing his usual cowboy boots, she was several inches taller in her stilt heels.

The wedding party left the upstate New York estate where the ceremony was held and drove to the River House for champagne toasts. The doorman sprang to open the door of the limousine and one of the male guests offered Helen his hand, Dr. James Monsour, Mike's cousin, recalled.

"May I help you, Mrs. Davis?" he asked.

"Don't you ever call me that!" she hissed at him.

Professionally, she was "Miss Helen Bonfils," and Miss Bonfils she would remain.

When the couple married, Mike was twenty-eight; Helen was sixty-nine, information she considered no one's business but her own.

Helen put off telling Hoyt of the marriage until May 1. When she called him from New York, she told him she thought he should know, but that nothing should appear in the paper. Ep argued

Papa's Girl

Tiger Mike in his office in the First National Bank, surrounded by oil core samples. Staked by Helen, he made a fortune.

Courtesy of The Denver Post.

vehemently with her—something he rarely did—saying her marriage was news and should be reported in *The Post*. "My God, Helen," he told her, "it's just a matter of time 'til the *News* has the story." That settled it. Reluctantly, she agreed.

That afternoon, a brief story appeared below the fold on the front page of *The Denver Post*:

> *Miss Bonfils Married to Oil Man.*
> *Announcement was made Friday of the marriage of Miss Helen G. Bonfils, prominent in theater circles in New York and Denver, and Mike Davis, Denver oil man. They were married April 2.*
>
> *The marriage ceremony was performed at the Frank Gould estate at Irvington-on-Hudson. Attending were Robert L. Reed, general counsel for the Sun Oil Company, and Mrs. Reed.*

Papa's Girl

> *The party was entertained at dinner later by Mr. and Mrs. Reed at the Ardsley Country Club.*
>
> *Mr. Davis is the owner of the Tiger Oil Company with offices in the First National Bank building and is associated with Miss Bonfils and Haila Stoddard in the production of* Come Play With Me *which opened at the York Theatre in New York City Thursday night.*

The story hit Denver like a small tornado. Few people, outside of a handful of close friends and Helen's family of servants, even knew she had been seeing Mike. Some found it strange that the story made no mention of Helen's affiliation with *The Post*. But most of all, everyone wondered about this mysterious bridegroom.

ATWILL GILMAN
Helen's Friend

The morning after the marriage was announced, I called at the Sherman Plaza apartments to take Benecia Batione to church. Miss Batione was a maiden lady, very well born, who earned a modest living by giving Spanish lessons to Denver society ladies. She was one of a number of financially strapped elderly ladies who Helen Bonfils helped on a regular basis, and a friend of many years.

When Miss Batione stepped from the elevator into the lobby, I had never seen anyone look so distressed.

"Is anything wrong?" I asked.

"Have you seen this morning's *News*?" she asked. The *News* had jubilantly splashed its account across the front page, and it was in no way as subdued as *The Post*'s report.

"Helen has let us all down," Miss Batione said grimly. "Had she been a drinking woman, I would have said she was drunk. But she doesn't drink, so there is *no* excuse for it."

DR. FRANK MCGLONE
Helen's Physician

I know Helen didn't have any intention of marrying Mike the day before the wedding. Dr. Frode Jensen, who took care of her in New

York, told me Mike came over that day and said if Frode didn't encourage Helen to marry him he was going to jump out the window. And Frode went over and opened the window.

I had hoped she would marry Cyril Ritchard, the British actor. He had directed her in *Arms and the Man* for the Brattle Theatre in Boston, and they saw each other socially in Denver and New York. They made a handsome couple and seemed to enjoy each other's company.

When Helen returned to Denver in June, she was confronted everywhere by what seemed to her a townful of "Nosy Parkers."

Everywhere she turned, she encountered questioning looks and sidelong glances, even when people were too tactful to press

Left to right, former heavyweight boxing champ Jack Dempsey, Helen's bodyguard Mike Carroll, Tiger Oil geologist Walt Dahmer and Tiger Mike Davis at Dempsey's New York night club.

Courtesy of Mike Carroll.

her for details. Helen had never been one to concern herself with what others thought of her actions. Neither was she accustomed to having to explain herself, but, now, some people felt entitled to explanations.

Arnold Gurtler was one. George and Helen had been married in the Gurtler home all those years ago, and the Gurtler brothers owned Elitch's where she began her professional career as an actress and where George directed for eighteen years.

A short while before, when *The Post* reported that Mike was in partnership with Haila and Helen in producing *Come Play With Me*, the blunt Arnold felt entitled to confront her. "Who is this Mike Davis?" he persisted.

"Oh, he's just a businessman, an acquaintance of mine," she had replied airily.

Now that their marriage had been announced, Arnold, looking even more Teutonically puzzled, once more prodded Helen with his questions. "It's a business arrangement," Helen said dismissively. "My only true love was George."

Gretchen Weber of *The Post*, always forthright, was equally candid: "Helen, why did you do it?"

"Oh, Gretchie," she sighed, "loneliness is a terrible thing."

At a party a woman gushed to her, "Helen, dear, I'm so glad you have someone to take care of you!"

Helen bristled. "I don't need anyone to take care of me," she told the woman stiffly. And that was partially true.

CHAPTER TWENTY-THREE
MORE ABOUT MIKE

HAILA STODDARD
Actress, Friend

I first met Mike in the summer of 1956 when he was in uniform as Helen's chauffeur and he used to drive us places. Then George died, and whatever happened, Mike moved in. It was one of those times when I didn't know what was going on because it came as a great shock to me.

I went over to the River House and there was this young man, very nattily dressed in a beige gabardine suit. Helen said, "Haila, you remember Mike?"

And I said, "Oh—yes."

Soon afterwards, she told me, "Mike is doing such interesting things in the oil business. He really is an exceptional man, and I have such faith in him. He is so full of all the things he is doing, and he'd like to write a book with you." I dutifully listened to him, but he was just telling me his fantasies.

Then Helen called me over to the River House a few days after they were married to tell me the news. None of her friends had been

No one could tell Helen Bonfils what to do, ever.

invited to the ceremony, though she did include her "family," Fanny, Nora and Arthur.

Mike's cousin, Dr. James Monsour, who was as elegant as Mike was uncouth, was originally asked to be the best man. But, in the end, that part went to Robert Reed, general counsel for the Sun Oil Company. Helen realized the participation of the oil executive would add credence to Mike's stature as an "oil man" when the news had to get around.

She fell madly in love with Mike. She was so avid for him, she was enchanted. She actually became younger and she went out a lot more. She would run to meet Mike when he came into a room.

I think she was a highly sexed woman. She had been surrounded by homosexuals because they were harmless. Daddy didn't question her choice of them as companions because he was a very smart man. Mike awoke her sexually.

The basis of Mike's attraction for her was that he reminded her of Papa. Mike is totally ruthless, and Helen often told me, "If you put Papa down in the middle of a desert, he'd make money." She used to tell me these hair-raising tales about Papa without a note of criticism. If you had to be a little ruthless, quite a little devious, in fact—well, those are the rules of the game.

Ever since we used to exchange confidences in the dressing room at Elitch's, I had been aware of her very sensual nature. I think because sex was forbidden to her, that's why she liked to talk about it. It would sort of titillate her.

Helen was really fascinated by a kind of bathroom talk, a kind of anatomical talk—"how do you suppose they do it?"—that didn't interest me. I used to tune her out. I wish now I'd listened more. I might have understood her better.

But, as for marrying Mike, Helen never did anything she didn't want to. A lot of people thought they could pull the wool over her eyes, but she was a very bright woman, and she only allowed herself to be duped when she wanted to be.

DR. FRANK MCGLONE
Helen's Physician

No one knew why she married Mike. She never liked him. He was like a child; he would go into tantrums. I used to take care of Mike when he was Helen's chauffeur. Once several nuns in full habit were visiting the mansion. Mike was purposely hollering and using the foulest language in a room next door. Then he came in, in just his undershorts. He did things to shock people and this embarrassed Helen.

I saw Mike come in one time with a check for $25 million he got from wells in Montana. He gave Phyllis McGuire half of the millions and built her a home in Las Vegas.

Nobody could believe he could do the things he did. Helen was hearing all these things—that he put $10,000 worth of flowers on a plane Phyllis was going to ride in. He'd talk about bringing her into the house to live.

I finally cornered Mike; he wasn't a real big guy and I had played football at the University of Colorado. I grabbed him by the collar and said, "You've got to quit doing these things." I told Helen and she said she was glad someone had told him to behave.

HAILA STODDARD
Actress, Friend

Helen loved the fact that Mike had enough guts to behave outrageously and, on the other hand, it repelled her. She was not embarrassed by anything. She was interested to see how badly he would behave and she sized people up by how they reacted to him.

Up until the day they were married he was one kind of person, and the day after, another. He just became very Sicilian. I thought, "She's going to be miserable." But he became like Papa to her. She tried to outwit him. She knew he was inferior as far as morality and ethics were concerned. She was denigrating Papa. It was a love-hate relationship.

He had no culture whatsoever, or refinement, or respect for anyone. He was a diamond in the rough who just wanted to get rougher. He was fascinated with gamblers and Las Vegas. He lost millions in the oil business before he made a quarter. When he lost, it was their money. When he made it all back, it was his.

He's not smart enough to be cruel. He's just mean. I stayed in the house a lot. I'd go into her room in the morning, and he'd chew her out just as a top sergeant would chew out a private. But I thought, "She's just sitting there thinking about how to get even."

She was playing a very dangerous game with him, and in a way she liked it. I always felt that to her it was worth it. She always wanted to see if she couldn't beat him at the game.

If someone wanted to get her attention, they wouldn't get it by being good and pious; she'd like them for being unconventional. I think she always liked slightly unconventional, on-the-racy-side people, rather than the proper citizens.

After we became partners in *The Thurber Carnival*, Mike was jealous of the money she was investing in it. I'd come to see her, and she might say to me in front of him, "Here's a book I think you'll like." And in it she would have tucked a check for twenty-five-thousand dollars.

She was the only devious woman I ever liked. She used to say to me, "I like you because you think like a man." Helen would not have been a supporter of women's rights. She wanted to be the only woman.

JERRY MIDDLETON
Mike's Barber

I call myself "Barber to the Stars" because I have cut hair for well-known men from Supreme Court Justice Byron White to (Denver) Mayor John Hickenlooper. I have a shop in the First National Bank Building where Mike had his offices and he became a client and good friend.

When I was widowed, Helen would often invite me for dinner. Then, after I remarried, my wife Sandy and I and Mike and Helen used to go out for dinner and to a movie or play every week when Mike was in town. Helen loved him so much. And he loved her. He used to call her "my golden palomino." I've read *Timberline* by Gene Fowler, and I think she loved Mike because he reminded her of her father. She was daddy's little girl.

We were invited to the Rose Hospital dinner at the Hilton Hotel when Helen was receiving an award. Helen was sitting on the dais. After dinner, the back door of the ballroom opened and Mike came in with Phyllis McGuire. She was wearing a glittery top and she looked so pretty. Helen was introduced and before she acknowledged the mayor or the governor or anyone, she said, "I want all of you here tonight to meet my dear friend, Phyllis McGuire of the singing McGuire Sisters." Sometimes we would be at Helen's house, and Phyllis would sing.

CHAPTER TWENTY-FOUR
AN HEIR APPARENT

May's long-ago taunt during their court battle about her sister's "lack of issue" always rankled. Although Helen's marriage to a younger man had brought a euphoric surge of vigor, the fact was that she was approaching her seventieth birthday in 1959 without an heir.

Her union merely complicated the problem of succession. Word had come back to executives at *The Post* that her cocky young husband was introducing himself around Las Vegas as "the owner of *The Denver Post*." They passed the word along to Helen in tones of obvious disapproval.

Here Helen drew the line: Papa's paper could not be allowed to fall into Mike's hands. It must continue under the control of knowledgeable professionals. Helen was almost seventy, and Palmer was nearing sixty. Who would carry on?

Helen had always been partial to the masculine sex, including male children. One of her favorites was Haila's son, Christopher Kirkland.

And so, one spring afternoon in 1959, she sent Joe Farrow, the chauffeur Mike had hired to replace himself, to Stapleton Airport to meet Chris, now a seventeen-year-old.

"Master Christopher! Welcome!" Arthur, the butler, exclaimed when the youth arrived. At the head of the stairway, Helen appeared in a peignoir as Fanny, her maid, and Nora, the cook, chirped in a chorus of Irish excitement. They had all known Christoper since he was a little boy, when, from a window seat in the River House apartment, he watched the boats on the East River, fascinated, while Haila and Whit had cocktails and Helen sipped tea.

He arrived in Denver the summer before he entered Harvard, for which Helen had insisted on paying his $1,500 tuition. He was to be a copy boy at *The Post* that summer.

Chris's father, Jack Kirkland, Haila's third husband, had been a newspaperman, and when Helen learned Chris wanted to follow in his footsteps, she persuaded him that he must begin his career at *The Post*. And, of course, she said, Chris must live with her and Mike during his internship.

CHRISTOPHER KIRKLAND
Haila's son

That first summer at *The Post* went by almost as fast as the newspaper's presses spun off the various editions in a blur of black and white. I was usually on the run, to the sports department, to the women's section, to the library, picking up copy, delivering photographs; to the backshop, where the editors stood around trays of lead type overseeing the makeup of the day's editions; then, several times a day, circling the building's five floors to deliver the editions the presses kept spewing forth, to the various departments.

On my day off I went to the horse races with Arthur, the butler, who was a great guy. Sometimes Helen and I went to the opening nights at Elitch's and to operas at Central City and the end-of-season play, a hit Broadway production that Helen had arranged to bring to the old mining town.

Sometimes we would go to a little Italian storefront restaurant in North Denver, a real people place. In all the times I had dinner with Helen at home, we never ate in the dining room; it was always with Nora and Fanny and Arthur in the dining nook off the kitchen. And we never ate out at a formal restaurant. It was always a Mexican cafe or a North Denver Italian place.

Mike was seldom around; he was out in the field most of the time. After I got to know him, I was relieved that he was away as often as he was.

I was put up in grand style in the Versailles Room. This was a luxury I concealed from my fellow copy boys at *The Denver Post*. I also found out that Helen was "Miss Helen" to almost everyone at *The Post*, except the senior editors.

Leaving for work early in the morning I would wave goodbye to Helen, who was quite a vision as she stood on the veranda adjoining her upstairs bedroom, wearing a peignoir, and directing the spray of a long watering hose at the flower beds in the front yard.

After a few days at *The Post* I told Helen that because I was the new kid in town I was working Sundays and it was kind of dull, but I didn't mind because I was getting to know a few people there. The second week, the head copy boy Dave Buresh (who later became a very good news photographer) called me over and said with some perplexity, "Word has come down; you don't work on Sundays."

Helen went to her office at *The Post* every day when she was in town unless her phlebitis was especially troublesome. She followed the routine she and George had established of spending as much of the fall and winter in New York as her health permitted.

She liked to go home about mid-afternoon, and I was usually finished after I delivered the Financial Final around to the various floors at about 3:45. Joe Farrow, who doubled as the doorman at the Bonfils Theatre, would pick us up in the little Ford sedan, and we would drive around town and look at her projects.

She'd had a playground made for kids and she liked to drive by and see them playing. And she owned several apartment buildings where she housed a number of old friends for little or no rent. I didn't realize until later she was looking after her philanthropies. When rehearsals for *The Denver Post* Opera began, we would go out to Cheesman Park to check on the progress of the production.

I remember one afternoon I burst into her boudoir. Two bricks elevated the front posts of her bed and relieved the discomfort of her phlebitis.

"I just read the greatest book!" I exclaimed.

"What was it, dear?" she asked.

"*Timberline* by Gene Fowler."

There was a stony silence. Helen sighed, "I don't know why he had to say all those horrible things about Papa. Papa was always good to him."

Throughout my undergraduate years at Harvard I continued to spend my summers in Denver. I went from being a copy boy to a sportswriter on *The Post*. In the summer of 1963, I committed a more serious gaffe. I had met the advertising director of the *Paris Tribune* at *The Denver Post* Opera. He was looking for an employee who might help breach the gap between the editorial and advertising realms at the *Tribune*—that is, someone with editorial experience who might cover some of the more commercial aspects of Parisian life, such as the fashion industry.

The next day, a Saturday, I had lunch with the man at the Brown Palace Hotel. When I went back to finish my shift at *The Post*, I was walking on air. I could hardly wait to tell Helen. I went to her boudoir as soon as I got home.

"You know," I said, "my father worked on the *Paris Tribune* and now I have a chance to do the same."

And Helen just froze. She thought I was doing just fine, going to college and working summers on *The Post*. I had already accepted the guy's offer and I had told everyone. But I felt very badly that I had kind of betrayed Helen. I have always felt that she was a kind of scholarship, putting me through fancy schools. She was so lavishly generous, and I was so thoroughly fond of her; the slightest thing I did to displease her was a great regret.

Even though Mike wasn't around often, his irregular visits became more than I could tolerate.

I remember him bringing home core samples from the field. We were in the grand living room—one of the few times we were in there—and he had these great cylinders of rock he was banging down on the piano and saying, "Smell that son of a bitch!" And, sure enough, it smelled like oil.

Helen's and Mike's bedrooms were at opposite ends of the upstairs and a world apart. Hers was full of memorabilia, pleasing colors, and light and airy. His was full of suits. I never did understand the attraction, his hold on her, or his power. He could get what he wanted.

I remember great stomach-turning scenes when he would flatter up to Helen and coo until he got what he wanted. And then there were other times when he was just rude and nasty, trying to push her around and embarrass her in front of me.

I think Mike was very abusive to Helen verbally. The cook and the butler and the maid and the little dog would just rise up against him. I remember the cook threatening once that if Mike didn't cut it out she was just going to crown him with a frying pan. He had been one of them ...

Finally, Helen just wanted to get rid of him, to see him get on a plane to Las Vegas. I think in the back of my mind I felt that if I got out he might not behave so badly toward her. I always felt so tenderly about her. I moved to my own small apartment.

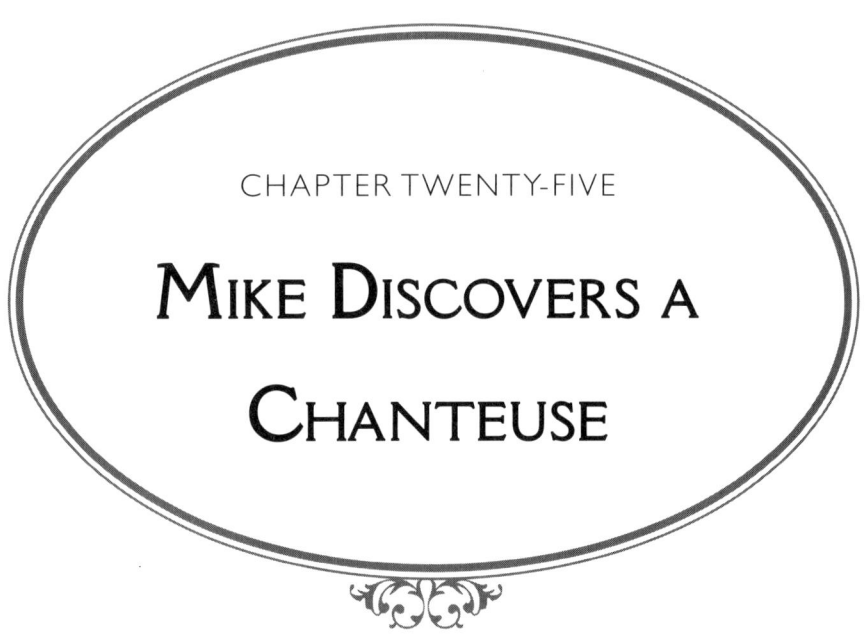

CHAPTER TWENTY-FIVE

MIKE DISCOVERS A CHANTEUSE

Mike took the oil business very seriously, and he did make millions. If Helen had any doubts about his success, all she had to do was read the newspapers. In 1967, *The Post* reported that he had discovered an oil field in southeast Montana, which, it said, "may be the biggest find in the Rockies in more than five years."

One day in 1968, he gleefully waved a copy of *Cervi's Rocky Mountain Business Journal* in front of his wife. The featured story read: "The time has come to stop calling him Mr. Helen Bonfils and to start calling her Mrs. Edward M. Davis." (Helen's reaction to that can only be imagined.) The article said, "The Tiger sold his recently found Montana oil wells and known reserves for no less than a conservative 25 million in cash or near-cash. That could be a low guess."

A year later the newspapers were reporting that Koch Exploration had signed an agreement to acquire more than 1.5 million acres of oil and gas in three states from Davis. In 1979, *Fortune Magazine* would name the former truck driver and grade-school drop-out a member of "The New Rich," those worth 50 million or more.

Helen knew little about the oil business except what Mike told her. It was a costly education. The drilling rigs and inland drilling barge, the private plane and other trappings, cost her $7 million before Mike ever made a dollar.

But it wasn't all work for Mike. On one of his trips to Las Vegas he met Phyllis McGuire, a very attractive blonde and one of the famous singing McGuire Sisters. Phyllis, Dorothy, and Christine got their start on *The Arthur Godfrey Talent Show*. The three girls had been singing together since Phyllis was four years old.

Mike developed a seemingly insatiable appetite for young Phyllis. Helen knew all about it, because he told her about Phyllis— in glowing terms.

"I want my little Sweetie (that was Helen) to meet Phyllis," he said. "She's a wonderful girl; you'll love her. Will you invite her to visit? Please?"

Of course. Helen got on the phone and invited Phyllis to visit. Arrangements were made for the singer to stay at the Lido Apartments, just down the street from the big house. Helen found Phyllis to be

Denver Jeweler Jess Kortz, Phyllis McGuire and Helen Bonfils at an awards banquet in 1957.

Photo courtesy of Jess Kortz.

everything Mike said, and more. Phyllis was "friendly, funny, gracious, totally enthusiastic and very, very pretty," as Dominick Dunne described her in his article in *Vanity Fair* in June 1989, "The Biggest Jewels in Las Vegas."

And Phyllis told people, "Helen Bonfils is the finest woman I've ever known."

MIKE CARROLL
Helen's Bodyguard

All Mike wanted to do was work, work, work. But then he met Phyllis McGuire, and he did make time for her. That meant less time for Helen.

Tiger Mike and Phyllis were introduced by Nat King Cole's bodyguard in 1960, a year after Miss Helen and Mike got married. Mike fell for her right away, but Phyllis did her best to discourage him because her regular boyfriend was "Momo" Salvatore Giancana. Momo was a major Mafia figure, about twenty years older than Phyllis.

He was the successor to Al Capone, and was a top member of La Cosa Nostra, the national crime syndicate. It was said that he sat in the Armory Lounge in Forest Park, Illinois, and ordered killings just as easily as he ordered linguini.

He owned points in the biggest Las Vegas casinos, the Riviera, the Desert Inn, and the Stardust, and I've heard his "business interests" in the United States and Central and South America brought in an annual take of $40 million to $50 million.

Phyllis pulled Mike behind a slot machine and warned him, "Look, do you want to end up at the bottom of Lake Mead? Because I've got a boyfriend and he doesn't like competition."

But then Giancana took himself out of the picture. He exiled himself to Mexico after he was the subject of a federal grand jury hearing in 1965. Mike moved in when Momo moved out. He built Phyllis a fantastic house in Las Vegas.

Phyllis was very good to me; I had a new Lincoln to drive around when I was in Las Vegas. Mike would tell me to keep an eye on her after her show, but she would dismiss me.

URSULA SIEVERS
Helen's Private Nurse

People were always asking Miss Helen how she could put up with Mike's running after Phyllis, and she would just say, "She keeps him out of my hair, if nothing else."

HAILA STODDARD
Actress, Friend

Once I asked Helen point-blank, "Helen, how can you just sit there and watch Mike carry on with Phyllis—right under your nose?"

She sighed and said, "Oh, honey, he's young and he's got to have someone ..."

CHAPTER TWENTY-SIX

SUCCESS AT LAST

ABOUT HELEN

The preparation of Haila's musical for its Broadway debut became so all-engrossing and time-consuming that Helen had little time to dwell on Mike's frequent absences.

A Thurber Carnival opened in New York's ANTA Theatre on February 26, 1960. The next day, the Associated Press reported, "In a rare happening on Broadway, all of the major Broadway critics were wholeheartedly enthusiastic."

Brooks Atkinson of the *New York Times* said it was "the freshest, funniest show of the year"; the *Herald Tribune's* Walter Kerr found it a "completely captivating revue." In the *Daily News*, John Chapman told readers, "Anybody who shuns this house of laughter is crazy."

Helen devoured the reviews. She couldn't get enough of them, re-reading every sentence to make sure there was no mistake, that she had a real, standing-room-only hit on her hands. At last! For so long the reviews had mostly ranged from tepid to unkind (except for the ones dear Betty Craig rewrote for *The Post*, of course.)

Papa's Girl

Was she pleased? Hell, yes! as Mike would say. Success is the sweetest revenge. She might still be Mrs. Moneybags, but now she had earned Broadway's respect.

The Associated Press dispatch went on to report, "To the native American humor which Thurber brought to the pages of the *New Yorker* ... has been added the producing know-how of Michael Davis, Helen Bonfils and Haila Stoddard, the directorial perception of Burgess Meredith and acting skills of Tom Ewell, Paul Ford and Peggy Cass."

Musical comedy star Ethel Merman with Helen Bonfils. Helen adored theater people.
Courtesy of The Denver Post.

"The know-how of Michael Davis" was a joke among insiders. Mike had insisted on being part of the production. Haila agreed reluctantly, but protested, "Mike, your name can't come before Helen's in the credits; it just isn't right."

"I don't give a good Goddamn," Mike insisted stubbornly. "My name's gonna come first."

And Helen said to Haila, "Oh, honey, let it go; it won't do any harm."

HAILA STODDARD
Actress, Friend

Helen had asked me to take Mike in as a partner because he was making all kinds of fuss. He had heard about "the ice." The ice is the block of choice tickets a producer receives to give or sell to friends and acquaintances. Mike thought the producer could go in and say, "I want one hundred tickets," and sell them for fifty dollars apiece. Mike never missed anything that concerned making a buck.

Helen had learned about the ice shortly before *Carnival* opened in Boston. The general manager came to Helen and me and asked, "What do you want to do about the ice?"

Helen didn't understand. "Do you mean we have to pay for the air conditioning, too?" she asked. In those days, clumps of ice were set around the theater and fans blew over them, cooling the theater. So she was set straight on the meaning.

Because of Helen's backing, no expense was spared in getting *Carnival* right. We were able to have nine weeks out of town. Helen went with us. We opened in Columbus and played St. Louis, Cleveland, and Cincinnati. Of course, we had our ups and downs.

One snag concerned the revolving sets and a treadmill which seemed to float—or, at least, that was the concept—across the stage, carrying a quartet of musicians playing an original jazz score by Don Elliott.

In Philadelphia, a man called who said he liked the show so much, but that we had a noisy treadmill.

I said, "I know, and we're at our wit's end about it."

"I can build you a quiet one, but it will be expensive," he said. It turned out that his specialty was constructing the revolving bases used to display refrigerators on television commercials. He got the job of building a quiet treadmill, and he did that.

Helen had requested her favorite designer, Elinor Jenkins, as the costume designer. They just loved dressing up, Elinor and Helen. Elinor's clothes were wonderful, but of such a different era than my idea of style. I had a concept of the costumes that would be very simple because of the Thurber line drawings which were used for backgrounds. There would be a costume, I thought, like a sack with different accessories to denote the different characters.

Elinor tried to do that, and she did it extremely well. Helen got upset because she thought they were too plain. She just loved furs, jewelry, and high heels.

Elinor got marvelous notices for the witty costumes, but Helen came to me and pleaded, "Can't we just dress them up a little bit?"

"Of course," I said.

But Helen wasn't a singer, and after the changes we got calls from the actresses saying the numbers weren't going too well because of all the glittery encumbrances. They had put a wide rhinestone belt on Alice Ghostley, for example, and she was unhappy about it.

We worked out a compromise. We did a color wash over the background—the Thurber line drawings—to coordinate with one color in the costumes. And once it became colorful, Helen was happy. And she was right about it.

ELINOR JENKINS
Designer

I met Helen Bonfils and George Somnes after World War II when I had a design studio at 52nd Street and Fifth Avenue. This beautiful woman swept in with this handsome man. He looked like John Barrymore. She exclaimed, "Darling! At last I've found you."

We had never met before, but she was so affectionate.

She had been buying my things at a shop in Chicago, but they took the labels out so she didn't know who the designer was. But one time they forgot to do this, and she saw "Elinor Jenkins" and found me in New York.

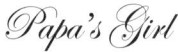

This was the early 1950s when American women did not yet have access to French designers. My husband, Frank, and I had an atelier with a lovely stairway that models would sweep down.

We had become well known on Broadway because we did the costumes for many productions. I dressed Ethel Merman for *Anything Goes* and, later, I did the costumes for Mary Martin, including the little fur coat she wore when she sang *My Heart Belongs to Daddy*.

Helen was a very private person; she didn't have many close friends. But she was a beautiful person, a philanthropist. She would pick up animals off the street and take them to her apartment in the River House. She would invite out-of-work actors for a meal.

Frank and I visited her in Denver. After Frank died, Helen and I became the closest of friends. We would go to openings and sit in the back row. She was a very private person.

I plan to write a book—I'll call it *Take Off Your Clothes*—and I will dedicate it to Helen, "my favorite person." I will use her picture as the frontispiece, one in which she is wearing her favorite sort of dress, black with a touch of white.

Chapter Twenty-Seven

The Family

"Loneliness is a terrible thing," Helen had told her friend Gretchen Weber when she was asked why she remarried. Soon enough, Helen found that marriage didn't change things much. Mike was so busy pursuing his oil deals in Wyoming—and his chanteuse in Las Vegas—that he was away most of the time.

So, as before, Helen had her "family": Fanny, her longtime maid; Nora Leyden, the housekeeper; Arthur, the butler; her day and night nurses, Ursula Sievers and Joyce Merlino; and her security man, Mike Carroll.

It was after George's death in 1952 that Palmer Hoyt insisted Helen get a bodyguard. For a recommendation he turned to Jack Carberry, *The Post*'s gravelly-voiced sports editor and onetime police reporter who knew Denver seamy-side out. Jack, who was also a dear friend of Helen's, recommended an investigator on District Attorney Bert Keating's staff for the job. Mike Carroll was six-foot-three inches of burly strength and affable Irish charm, a cop's cop with a tender heart and a gift of gab.

Helen had known Mike when he moonlighted as a special officer at Elitch Gardens. He had even played walk-on roles when a play called for a uniformed policeman. She was always most comfortable with

employees who were familiar to her, so if she had to have a bodyguard, she was pleased to have Mike Carroll. After her marriage to Mike Davis, Mike Carroll often served as his bodyguard as well.

MIKE CARROLL
Helen's Bodyguard

Palmer Hoyt's instructions to me were, "Don't you ever leave this woman." I was with her until her death twenty years later. I dearly loved Miss Helen; she was the light of my life. She was the greatest thing that ever happened to me; she changed me from a half-assed gangster to a gentleman.

I had grown up in a rough North Denver neighborhood. When I entered her employ, I moved into a mansion and became a part of a household with servants and all the trappings. Miss Helen arranged for me to be fitted with black tie and white-tie evening dress for the times when I accompanied her to opening nights and social events in New York.

For several years I spent every night at the mansion at 707 Washington Street and my days on duty with the district attorney's office. When my wife complained that she never saw me, I arranged for another investigator on the district attorney's staff, Jim Turner, to relieve me at Miss Helen's on weekends.

At first the servants were polite but pretty distant. Fanny had been Belle Bonfils' maid before she became Helen's. Arthur had joined the staff as George's valet; Norah Leyden, the housekeeper, and Mary, the cook, had also been in Helen's household for a number of years. They were mostly Irish, except for Arthur, who was English. "Mr. Coddle," the women called me, because they couldn't say Carroll.

One night I heard groaning from the five-room suite where the staff lived. Fanny was doubled up in bed. I put a robe around her and carried her out to my police car. I took her over to St. Joseph's Hospital with the siren on. Attendants met me at the emergency entrance and half an hour later she was operated on. It was appendicitis, real bad.

After that, Mike Carroll got to be a great guy. Before, I'd walk in and they'd stop talking. I was an outcast. They thought I was a spy.

But after that night they thought I'd saved Fanny's life and I could sit there at the table and b.s. with them.

Mike was away, finding oil wells and drilling most of the time, and the servants were Miss Helen's family. Unless she was dining out, she ate with them in the dining nook off the kitchen. That's where we celebrated St. Patrick's Day with corned beef and cabbage and drinks for everyone, including Father Anderson, Dr. McGlone, the staff, her nurses and any old friends who happened to stop by. Helen would have soda with a twist of lemon, and Joe Farrow and I would have ginger ale.

I would sing *When Irish Eyes are Smiling* and *Sweet Rosie O'Grady*. I had a tenor voice that had got me a scholarship to Denver's Cathedral High School.

When Mike Davis became an oil man, he picked Joe Farrow as his replacement as Miss Helen's chauffeur. Joe was black, a very likable guy who had been the elevator operator at the First National Bank building where Mike had his office. Joe's barbequed ribs and chicken were some of the family's favorite food.

Sometimes I took Miss Helen out to my old North Denver neighborhood for dinner at Gaetano's. The restaurant was the supposed hub of Mafia activity in Denver, and its Italian food was good. Miss Helen liked the idea of rubbing elbows with guys who might be gangsters. The Smaldones, who owned the restaurant (and were sometimes mentioned in *The Denver Post* in not-too-flattering terms), had been friends of mine since childhood.

Miss Helen liked simple things. She loved popcorn, which I would bring her at Elitch's. She kept her handkerchief wrapped around the popcorn box. She was the most elegant woman I've ever been around in my life. She loved to ride trains—going through the little towns and hearing the whistles. Penny candy. The smallest things in life thrilled this woman.

Palmer Hoyt saw that I had an allowance to make up for her—well—stinginess in tipping. At the airport she would graciously hand a dollar bill to a skycap who was juggling two carts piled high with luggage. I would slip him another ten dollars.

Her father had been so afraid she would be kidnapped that he never let her go out with anyone. So she hadn't had much experience with men when she married after her parents' deaths.

I was with her when they finally settled the family will. I said, "I saw your sister's picture in the paper today." She said, "Mike, darling, I have no sister. Let's don't discuss it again." She hated May's guts. May married a drape hanger and they lived in a mansion in Jefferson County.

In New York I would escort Miss Helen to the theater in my formal dress. A lot of times she would be opening plays. Of course, she closed a few, too. At the theater, all the would-be actors would want to hang around her. She'd talk to everyone, and after they left, she'd say, "Mike, darling, who was that?"

I got my share of attention, too. Aspiring actors and playwrights and producers would say to me, "Good evening, Mr. Bonfils."

Helen had a thing about having her picture taken. I think the photos showing the wrinkles and bags didn't match up with how she pictured herself. "I want no one taking my picture," she'd tell me. "Now, Mike, darling, if anyone does, take his camera away and I'll support you."

She got tired pretty easily. After the first act, she'd often say, "Michael, dear, take me home."

I had a room in the River House apartment. On nights when I was free, I'd visit Jack Dempsey, the former world's champion heavyweight boxer who grew up in Colorado and now owned a popular restaurant in midtown Manhattan. Or I might go to the boxing matches at Madison Square Garden, or take in a baseball game. It was a great life for a kid from North Denver.

In the Denver mansion, my room was next to Miss Helen's. Sometimes I'd hear her moving around at night. I'd knock on her door to check on her and find she was playing solitaire. "Oh, Mike, dear, come in and sit with me and tell me about when you were a boy," she'd say. I would sit with her and tell her stories about the North Side, where I was christened Clarence Leo Vincent Daniel Carroll. I was in more fights with that name.

During the Prohibition years, my friends and I would outsmart the North Denver bootleggers by swiping their kegs of beer and wine and hiding them in caves. I'd tell Miss Helen how my life changed when Monsignor Joseph Bosetti got me a scholarship to Cathedral High School so I could sing in the choir. It was the society school of Denver's Catholic schools, and when the East Denver kids sneered

Helen with *Denver Post* fashion editor Gretchen Weber, left, and symphony founder Helen Marie Black.

Helen Bonfils in her later years.

at me, I beat the shit out of them a couple of times. They got to respect me; I was a big kid.

Then I would show her the long scar on my arm from a knife slash a prostitute gave me when my partner and I were taking her to jail in our patrol car. And I would tell about the time I was shot twice in the chest. I would remember how I held my dying partner in my arms after a shoot-out.

Later, when I was directing traffic on Sixteenth Street, I was always polite to the little old ladies who would ask me where Neusteter's store was, even though they were standing right in front of it at the time.

"Mike, dear," Miss Helen would say, "you ought to write a book."

Thursday night was pinochle night. Miss Helen had the most beautiful gowns, and she'd wear a different one all the time. Miss Merino, the night nurse, and Miss Helen were partners, and Father Anderson and I were partners. If we played ten games, Father Anderson and I would win eight of them.

JOE FARROW
Chauffeur

I've been in the public eye so long I could look at a person and see whether I could get along with them. When it came to Miss Helen, the vibes was there. The lady impressed me so much.

I would drive her to *The Post* on the days she felt well enough to go to her office. Later in the afternoon, she might want to shop at Jonas Brother' Furs or Neusteter's, or Bohm Allen's jewelry store, to find a present for a friend. She always said she liked to patronize local merchants.

On Tuesday nights I drove her to opening nights at Elitch's Theatre. She always excused herself after the first act and retired to an office where she could prop her feet up and watch *Gunsmoke* or wrestling, her favorite TV programs.

I drove her to Fairmount Cemetery almost every day, to visit the crypts of her dearly departed, Mama, Papa, and George. Her sister May's large crypt stood across the way, apart from the family.

Papa's Girl

In July we would go every afternoon to Cheesman Park to check on the rehearsals of *The Denver Post* Opera. We also took a ride most every night, just her and me and Rosie, the mutt who was Miss Helen's favorite dog.

CHAPTER TWENTY-EIGHT
MISS HELEN AT HOME

URSULA LUJAN SIEVERS
Helen's Private Nurse

I was with Miss Helen five years, from 1967 until her death in St. Joseph's Hospital in June 1972. I had been manager of the nurses' pool at St. Joseph's, and I was between jobs when Mike Carroll called me. I had taken care of Mike's first wife. I didn't know from Adam who Helen Bonfils was. Oh, boy, did I have a lesson in life.

It was a stressful job for me because I was a young gung-ho nurse, and I found that things that should have been done were not being done. The first thing I saw when I went to work was Miss Helen sitting there eating chocolate-filled Bismarcks for breakfast. And she was a diabetic.

She was being allowed to do whatever she wished. The trouble was, she was a very strong person and a very lovable person. The other day nurse and I would keep her on a diabetic diet for eight hours, and then the night nurse would come on duty with a box of Mrs. See's chocolates. Finally, Miss Helen went into a diabetic coma.

Instead of taking her to the hospital, she talked us into treating her at home. Mike was letting her have her way.

She used to call me "Punk" and "Baby," because I was the youngest nurse on her staff. I used to dye her hair yellow blonde. I had more fun with that woman than I did with any girlfriend I ever had. She could be very funny, and she'd get us all laughing. But, often, I would come home tired because we'd do a lot of talking. We'd discuss religion and our perception of good and evil. She was a very wise woman; she understood people. She'd say, "It takes a smart man to gain a little bit of prosperity and not let it change him." And then she'd give me examples.

With Mike, there was love there. They'd sit down for dinner and he'd entertain her in a way no one else could. When I first came, he was there a lot. Then he was gone a lot—to Las Vegas, or wherever Phyllis was. He was home for Christmas Eve, but I don't think he was ever there for Christmas.

I really loved that woman. I worked every holiday because those were such bad times for her. I think she was one of the lonesomest people I ever met, and lonesomeness was new to me, because I was from a large family.

Mike never came back from his trips empty-handed. He'd have these fur-laden clothes with designer labels for her and caviar for the six dogs and six cats. Missy, a dog Mike got from the pound, ran the house.

As I say, there was love there, but more like a mother and son. I would never have said that to her, because she said she hated kids. Those animals came before people.

Miss Helen used to say the best times she ever had were when my mother and I would fix a Mexican dinner at my house. We would start cooking the day before, and she and Joe Farrow and Father Anderson would come, Miss Helen in her high heels and furs. She liked the chili bowl and the enchiladas.

She'd say, "You're lucky; you don't live in a big house, but you can feel the love."

Miss Helen used to say, "If only someone would do something for me because of who I am and not for what I can do for them."

Mike was always wanting more money to do his deals. Without exception, the people who came were looking for something. Father

John Anderson and Frank McGlone got anything they wanted. She loaned money to Dr. McGlone to build a clinic.

She would say, "I wish Johnny wasn't a priest," but she thought of him as a companion. He had a coat lined with black diamond mink she gave him. She used to write out check after check to him. Mike would say, "I'm sick of seeing that priest come out of your bedroom with lipstick smears on his face." Miss Helen always planted kisses on her friends and especially the men. There was always a lot of gossip. Nora and Fanny had her sleeping with Mike before Mr. Somnes died. Mike was giving her physically what she'd never had before.

When Mike was around, he'd put a stop to a lot of the crap going on in the house. I think he saved her life many times. He'd make everyone snap to and see that she was better cared for.

Mike used to go on one of his tirades and the next day, honest to God, she'd be better. She thrived on dissension. Nora and Fanny said Mike carried on like he did because that's what her father used to do. Sure, Mike was getting money from her, but at least he had a license. Because the others were more polished, does that make them any better than Mike Davis? He gave her more love and gratitude than she got from all those other people.

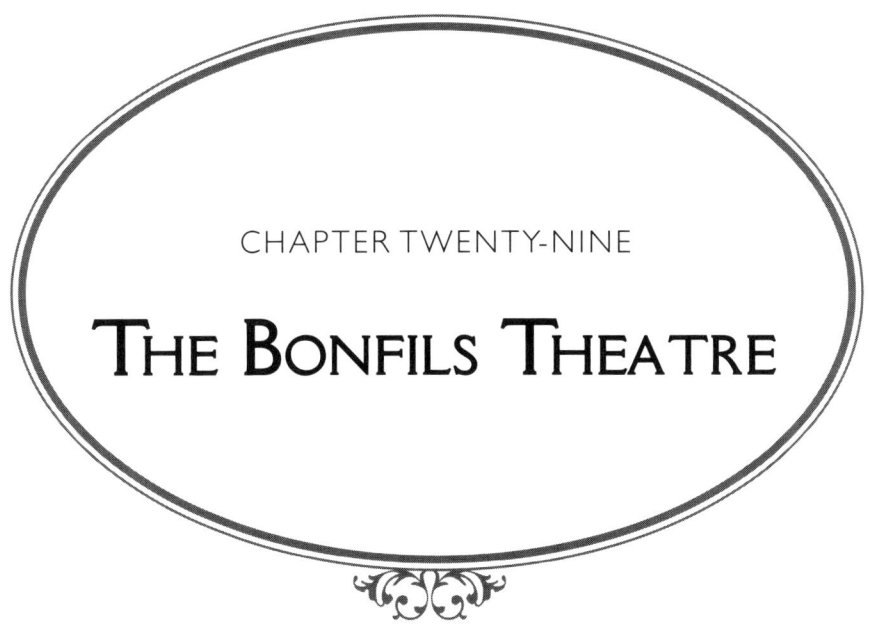

CHAPTER TWENTY-NINE
THE BONFILS THEATRE

By the early sixties, Helen's health curtailed her annual trips to Manhattan, where she had once spent half the year. In Denver, she spent fewer hours in her office at *The Post* and more time at home with the household staff.

Helen's salvation, in the years Mike was so often away, was the Bonfils Theatre. The Bonfils, as it was known, filled her time and gave her the pleasure of being involved in the theater with long-time friends she had known since her days with the Civic. Even in the years when she and George had spent most of their time in New York, she had never failed to appear in one production at the Bonfils each season.

In 1956, the year George died, she hired Henry Lowenstein as set director at the Bonfils. Her director was Harry Geldard, who, in Helen's view, was a divinely handsome, marvelously charming Englishman. When he entered a room, she said that "every woman present went into a swoon." Bradford Hatton, the son of her old friend, the actress Adele Hatton, was the theater's business manager. Dorothy Rader, whom Helen had known since her early days with the Denver Civic Theatre, was box office manager. She was comfortably surrounded by familiars whom she loved and enjoyed.

HENRY LOWENSTEIN
Set Director, the Bonfils Theatre

Harry Geldard was an honest-to-God alcoholic. When he was on a bender, we wouldn't see him for days at a time. When we did catch up with him, the only way to get him out of it was to sit with him constantly because he would drink hair tonic, rubbing alcohol—anything. You couldn't take your eyes off him. If I sat with him for thirty-six hours, he'd bounce out of bed like a fresh-born babe. I was exhausted.

Helen didn't have any tolerance for drunks, but she never saw him in his inebriated condition. He was a smooth man and he would prey on her when he was sober. I think he feathered his nest pretty well. Finally, I told Helen, "I'm leaving. I can't do this anymore. You've got to get rid of him or me."

Helen said, "Well, dear, if he promises to behave, can he work for you on one condition: If he takes one drink, he's out?" I agreed, but Geldard was soon off on another toot, and then he was gone.

MIMI HATTON
Bradford Hatton's wife

Helen Bonfils was not one of my favorite people. She was man crazy; she behaved in a way that was not at all suitable for a woman of her age.

I saw it with Mike Davis; how he would carry her up the steps to our house when we invited her for dinner while George was ill at home. How she would snuggle against him. He was strong as a bull. He was a very unsavory individual. She should never have married him.

And Geldard. She was reacting as a much younger woman to this man; she was obviously infatuated. She showered him with gifts—a cashmere coat, a watch, crystal highball glasses. And he would bring her tiny paper umbrellas from his drinks at Trader Vic's, which he would present in his suave manner, bowing from the waist.

Papa's Girl

HENRY LOWENSTEIN
Set Director, the Bonfils Theatre

I succeeded Geldard as director in 1967, and if something special was needed—parking lots, construction—Helen would make sure everything was done on a very businesslike basis. She was very generous in that sense.

I must say she was also very tight, but not in a nasty sense. There were people all over town she supported. Still, she never encouraged anyone to come to her for money, for the theater or anything else. I can say I never asked her for anything personally, and a hell of a lot of people did. I made it a principle. Here was this very wealthy woman; I loved her dearly and thought she was a wonderful person. I thought it would be unthinkable to go to her for anything except for the theater.

The only time she ever chewed me out was when I made a deal with a New York costume company in order to save the theater several thousand dollars.

"I don't care," Helen said. "You should have got the costumes in Denver. My money comes from the people of Denver and if you buy anything, you buy it here."

I found her totally knowledgeable about what she wanted. I had great respect for her. She was never a slouch about being daring. When we were considering doing *Boys in the Band*, a play with a homosexual theme, she said, "Let's shock them."

She wasn't easily fazed.

DOROTHY RADER
Bonfils Theatre Box Office Manager

My first memory of Helen Bonfils was seeing her driving around town in an electric car with her friend, Thelma Kolb. They were so young and gorgeous together, Helen, a blonde with porcelain white skin, and Thelma, who looked so Indian.

Then, we met when we were both in the University of Denver's Civic productions. I had minor parts when she was playing leads. We'd have a chance to sit and visit. She was so democratic. I think she could have been one of the great actresses if she had started sooner. She had peach blossom skin, and she had no false modesty.

I made up my mind when I came to work at the Bonfils that I wouldn't be a fawning person. I felt that everyone wanted something from her. But then Helen was hurt by what she thought was my coolness. "Are you mad at me?" she asked me one night. "All you do is speak to me. You never come down to my office to visit."

Helen was a teetotaler, except for an occasional glass of champagne. Once, in her office, we were spooning champagne over ice cream. "Oh, Dorothy," she said, "that champagne made me quite tiddly!"

She knew so many people from New York, and she would have lovely buffets for the Broadway casts appearing at the Denver Auditorium after their performances, and for the casts at Elitch's, too. Brad and I were always invited to the parties. I remember at one, she was taking a very pretty blonde singer around the room and introducing her as "my very dear friend, Phyllis McGuire."

She was very susceptible to being liked and there was one man, a director, at the Bonfils who took advantage of her. Once he got drunk on opening night and flew to Hawaii.

Helen had named Bradford Hatton, the son of her old friend, Adele, the business manager of the Bonfils. He did absolutely nothing and made twice as much money as I did. If he spent twenty minutes a day in the theater, that was good. I was actually shouldering many of Brad's duties and working seven days a week for relatively little pay. But when someone asked Helen about a raise for me, she said, "No, she's making enough money—for a woman."

At that, she felt more kindly toward me than most women. She could be an autocrat. She had me in tears many times. But she could be a very kind person and I had a great deal of sympathy for her. I remember once I stopped by her office and she was depressed and crying. "No one loves me for myself," she said. "Everyone wants something." I remember feeling so sorry. Here she had all this, and I felt she didn't have the happy life she wanted.

I was married when I was sixty-five. Helen never quite forgave me for leaving the theater when I married. She was never quite as cordial and close.

CHAPTER THIRTY

THE ANIMAL FAIR

SHEILA BISENIUS
Godchild

Everyone was appalled at how Helen let the pets run the household. I remember the constant presence of all her pets and how she would let them destroy the household. One mutt she kept in Denver would run away and it had a tag that said, "In case I am found, please put me in a cab to 707 Washington Street."

JOE FARROW
Chauffeur

There were three labs, two German shepherds and Rosie, a mutt. Mike Davis brought the labradors. Every time he went to Nebraska to visit his mother, he'd come back with a small one.

Miss Helen built a great big house in the back yard that had beds for all of them and air conditioning. Her friends called it "the chateau."

Nothing was too good for Miss Helen's pets, including flowers, a casket and interment in Denver's pet cemetery.

Courtesy of The Denver Post.

MIKE CARROLL
Bodyguard

There were also five cats. And when those dogs would come racing in, through the kitchen and the dining room, down the hall and up the stairs, those cats would run up the curtains.

I'd say, "Miss Helen, those cats are ruining this house."

"What have they done now?" she'd ask.

"They've shredded the curtains."

"Well, dear," she'd say, without even looking up from her newspaper, "just call so-and-so down at The Denver (Dry Goods Store) and order some more."

Papa's Girl

DOROTHY RADER
Bonfils Theatre Box Office Manager

One time Helen decided to have a birthday party for one of the big, black dogs, a labrador, I believe. The guests were her friend Selma Kolb, Brad Hatton, manager of the Bonfils Theatre, and me. I sent some flowers. Brad stopped by a butcher shop and got a big bone.

The servants had washed down the dog house for the occasion. Nora, Fanny, and Arthur appeared with large silver trays of fried eggs and bowls of milk. The dogs got so excited they just slurped the eggs up. They raced around and got wet and shook their coats, soaking all of us.

Then we went into the library. There was a big round coffee table with nuts and mints on it. Helen let the one dog who was having the birthday in. He stuck his nose in the sugar and cream and cookies.

Brad was the wise one; he said he'd have bourbon and water. I took a piece of gorgeous chocolate cake and I think I had one bite; the dog came and ate the rest of it. I had expected to go to my son's graduation from the party, but I had to go home and change because I was all wet.

Sometimes I would visit Helen in her upstairs bedroom. She had diabetes, but she always had a box of candy around and was always cheating a little bit. She had a mouse she called "Ep" (after the publisher of *The Post*) that frisked about on the balcony outside her boudoir. She would say, "Take these crumbs and Ep will get them."

URSULA SIEVERS
Helen's Private Nurse

Those animals came before people.

Chapter Thirty-One
Helen Takes Over Elitch's

In 1964, Helen's old friend, Arnold Gurtler, called on Helen in her boudoir.

He told her that Elitch's had been losing money hand over fist. For one thing, it was a resident company and these had become costly dinosaurs. Several years earlier, Helen had paid for a remodeling of the theater and she held a mortgage on it. Now Arnold was asking her to take it over altogether.

"If I don't, what will become of it?" she asked.

Arnold walked over to the window and gazed out. "I'll tear it down," he said.

For Helen, that was unthinkable. She asked Whit Connor, now a friend of almost a decade, to manage the theater. "He's level headed, he has good judgment, and I think he likes me," she told his wife, Haila Stoddard.

WHITFIELD CONNOR
Friend

I'd had those seasons at Elitch's as an actor, but I had no experience as a producer, so Helen went out on a limb in hiring me. Our relationship became all the closer because I stayed in her home during the theater's summer season. We would have coffee each morning in her boudoir and discuss the previous night's performance and what the day might bring.

One morning when we were going over the box office receipts, Tiger Mike appeared in the doorway. He was glowering. "We haven't said our prayers," he growled at Helen.

Helen seemed at a loss for words.

"Well," Mike said impatiently, "let's say our goddamn prayers; I've gotta get the hell outta here."

The theater made money that summer, and at the end of the season, Helen's auditor called me in. "Elitch's isn't supposed to make money," he told me. "It's a write-off."

CHAPTER THIRTY-TWO

ENTER DONALD SEAWELL

Mike lost interest in Broadway after "the ice" turned out to be only a minor perk. Haila and Helen were free to take another partner, one who might make a genuine contribution to their production team. In time, Mike would rue the day he left an opening for a man who would prove to be his most formidable rival.

At about the time *Carnival* opened, Samuel Newhouse, one of the country's most powerful newspaper publishers, showed an interest in acquiring *The Denver Post*. He arranged for an introduction to Helen through the columnist, Leonard Lyons. Mr. Newhouse's penchant for buying up newspapers alarmed Helen.

"Honey," she said to Haila, "I need a classy lawyer to take care of these Eastern rustlers."

Haila had first met Donald Seawell, a suave and charming North Carolinian, when he was negotiating a contract for an actress who played with her in the soap opera, *The Secret Storm*. The show had a tough producer and the actors needed a negotiator who could be equally unyielding.

Don won Haila's admiration when he told the producer, "Sir, I did not emigrate from North Caroline to reinstate slavery."

Papa's Girl

Courtly Southerner Donald Seawell became *The Denver Post's* center of power as president and chairman of the board.
Courtesy of The Denver Post.

"I thought anyone who said something like that was for me," Haila said. With Helen's permission, she asked Donald to negotiate the rights for *The Thurber Carnival*. "We all clicked so well we asked him to become our silent partner." Seawell explained that, because of the ethics of the legal profession, being a full partner might be construed as advertising.

At the same time, Helen's valued and faithful friend E. Ray Campbell, the *Post's* attorney, was showing signs of age. "I need a lawyer to handle other matters as well," she told Seawell. He agreed to help her in what would come to be known as "the battle for *The Denver Post*."

In 1959, Donald Seawell was forty-seven. He had been a member of General Dwight Eisenhower's select D-Day staff. He had been acting ambassador to France, a governor of England's Royal Shakespeare Theatre (only the second American in that position), and was for many years chairman of the American National Theatre and Academy.

Equally impressive—to Helen, at least—was his list of clients: Alfred Lunt and Lynn Fontanne, Noel Coward, the playwrights Howard Lindsay and Russell Crouse, Tallulah Bankhead, and other luminaries of the theater.

Seawell was a handsome man. There was a slight wave in his light brown hair, and his blue eyes could be merry as well as intense; he was trim and erect in his impeccably tailored Saville Row suits. He spoke with wit and knowledge in a pleasantly modulated voice that carried echoes of his North Carolina heritage. Helen basked in the glow he cast over the Bonfils-Stoddard association.

Thanks to Seawell's connections, Bonard—as the threesome called their new partnership—was able to bring the Royal Shakespeare Company over for its U.S. tour in *A Hollow Crown*. Paul Scofield played King Lear when the production opened the New York State Theatre at the Lincoln Center.

CHAPTER THIRTY-THREE
A NEW PARTNERSHIP

With the astonishing success of *The Thurber Carnival*, everything kept clicking into place for Helen on Broadway. After Seawell arranged for the presentation of the Royal Shakespeare Company in *The Hollow Crown*, she was considered a cultured angel as well as a savvy one.

Haila had always been an admirer of C.P. Snow, and after his *The End of the Affair* was a hit in London, Bonard Productions was able to bring it to New York. Don and Haila adored Noel Coward. Haila got to know the British playwright, actor and bon vivant when she appeared with Clifton Webb in Coward's *Blithe Spirit*, and Coward and Seawell were longtime friends. In 1962, Helen learned, they were dying to do Coward's *Sail Away*. It was an operetta, a love story, starring Elaine Stritch, and a satire on tourism—an operetta that couldn't make up its mind, as Helen saw it. Anything Coward did was an event, to hear him tell it, anyway. However, it did appear to many that his sophisticated, brittle wit was out of tune with the theater currents of the 1960s.

Coward felt it was the times, certainly not him, that were out of joint. And, Helen would have agreed with his pronouncement: "Pornography bores me. Squalor disgusts me. Garishness, vulgarity and commonness of mind offend me, and problems of social significance on the stage, unless superbly well presented, to me are the negation of entertainment."

HAILA STODDARD
Actress, Friend

Before they met, Helen and Noel had a mutual admiration society. The trouble arose when they got to know one another. Noel had been having trouble finding financing for *Sail Away*, but, as he wrote in his diary, which later was published: "Then we heard from Don Seawell that Helen Bonfils would finance the show entirely and put up $400,000 without batting an eyelid! She is apparently the third richest woman in America. Within an hour he telephoned to say that he had talked to her in Denver (which she practically owns) and that she said that as the show was mine he could have committed her without troubling to telephone! This, I must say, was one of the most gratifying compliments I have had for a long time."

But once they met, Helen and Noel never really hit it off. He was facetious and witty and tremendously sophisicated. She wasn't sophisticated, ever. She hated thin; he was too thin. Helen liked big silver fox furs, sequins, ruffles. He represented everything that was chic and svelte. He wouldn't eat anything that didn't quiver. She liked popcorn and hot dogs. In Boston, there was a blow-up. He was hurt; she thought he was condescending.

Reviews of *Sail Away* after the New York opening were "carping," Noel complained. But he conceded that the musical was not a smash hit. As he wrote in his diary on October 29, 1961: "The management, Haila and Don—Helen Bonfils doesn't count—are comparatively inexperienced. They love the show and are determined to do everything in their power to keep it on for a year at least; although, according to present box-office portents, it looks as though it won't last beyond May or June."

It wasn't true, that Helen Bonfils didn't matter, but she sensed his dismissiveness and she was deeply offended.

What caused Helen and me to stop producing? There has always been something strange about it, so I'm not going to mention names. Someone wanted her to do something else.

First, in about 1963, a friend of mine brought me *The Subject Was Roses*. Helen thought it was an off-Broadway show, unless we could get a star like Art Carney, who was then appearing in *The Honeymooners* on TV.

The author said he wouldn't let it be done off-Broadway unless he could have Jack Albertson, practically an unknown. So I lost it. Helen wouldn't budge on it, and the partnership meant more to me than any play. I let it go, and it was a great success. A year later I was presented with Harold Pinter's *The Birthday Party*, which was doing very well in London.

I went to Helen and said, "This is a wonderful play. Pinter is coming to this country and reading his poetry." She came to a reading, climbed all these steps, and met Pinter, and told him how thrilled she was. A week later she changed her mind. Someone wanted her to change her mind for his benefit.

I said, "Helen, this is the second time. The first time, the partnership meant more to me than the play. But this time you told Mr. Pinter you would do the play, so I am going to have to go ahead on my own."

She said, "Honey, I understand. We will always be friends. There are certain things you like, and certain things I like."

We always remained very close friends. I really loved her.

MORTON GOTTLIEB
Broadway Producer

I met Helen through the producer Gilbert Miller. She had known him since she was in her teens and they traveled together with the Sells-Floto Circus. I was Gilbert's general manager, and she got in touch with me when she wanted house seats, the choice seats, which are sold at the producer's discretion.

In 1948 and '49, she might have called me for tickets for *Edward My Son*, in the 1950s for *Gigi*, and the Cleopatras—*Antony and Cleopatra* and *Caesar and Cleopatra*—with Laurence Olivier and Vivien Leigh. She'd pick up the tickets and we'd talk. We got to know each other.

We got to know each other better when I was general manager for *Sail Away*. What happened was, she was very impressed with how

Papa's Girl

I was trying to save her money. I got both American Express and Cunard to pay for part of the scenery, and I promoted $100,000 in goods and chattel to pay for an opening night party, among other things.

One day she said to me, "I know you want to be a producer. You find a play, and I'll give you the money."

I found a play, *Enter Laughing*, and she was as good as her word. She remained a limited partner, and we did some flops and some successes. I used to go out and visit Denver all the time, to discuss theater business.

She was an amazing, marvelous, wonderful woman with great insight and perception and great knowledge of the theater—except in one instance. She hated a play I wanted to do, first titled *Who's Afraid of Stephen Sondheim?* then, *Anyone for Murder?*. Its title on the London stage was *Sleuth*. I wanted, naturally, to do it in America. In fact, I wanted to do it here first. But Helen could never get through the script.

Finally, I proposed that I find twenty-four other contributors as limited partners and that she not put up any money. But she remained my general partner, and I split the profits with her when it became one of the biggest commercial smash hits of the theater.

Sleuth went on to become a smash hit and a movie. It's played everywhere; it's still done, and money is still going to her estate. Helen never went to see *Sleuth* until it was presented at the Denver Civic Auditorium five or six months before her death. She left after the first act, but before she did, she said to me, "Darling, I don't know how you ever put that over on the world."

Her sense about things was usually very good. What was so ironic was that *Sleuth* was her only giant, smash hit that made millions, and she never finished reading the original script and never saw the second act.

We got along very, very well. We understood each other. She understood what I wanted to do. When someone tells you, "I know you want to produce plays; you go out and find one and I'll back you"—when someone tells you that—it makes you feel so wonderful that they have confidence in you. It was thrilling what she would do in her generosity.

We didn't have an unbroken string of successes, of course; *Come Live With Me*, starring Soupy Sales, closed after four peformances in 1967.

She and Gilbert Miller remained in touch until he died in 1969. They met when he was assistant press agent for the Sells-Floto Circus (which Bonfils and Tammen owned for a time.) I'd guess she was about fifteen and Gilbert, eighteen. Gilbert's father, who was a major producer of his day, had shipped him out of town to learn to be a publicist.

Helen and a friend, Selma Groth, were traveling with the circus that summer. She used to recall how wonderful it was to ride in the Pullman car, a castle of luxury on wheels. She rode an elephant in the parade through the streets of towns on the days the circus opened. And she played the role of the heroine in a melodrama they put on and found she loved acting.

Bonfils and Tammen purchased the circus because one day Helen's father said to her, "what would you like most in the world for your birthday?" and she said, "I'd love a circus!"

Gilbert's wife was the former Kitty Basche, daughter of a prominent New York banking family. Gilbert used to say to me, "Oh, if we only had Helen Bonfils' money, what Kitty and I could do!" And Helen would say to me, "If only I had Kitty and Gilbert's money, what I couldn't do!"

URSULA SIEVERS
Helen's Private Nurse

In Denver, Miss Helen would sneak off to the Original Mexican Cafe to meet one of her boyfriends, Mort Gottlieb. Fanny, her maid, and I would get this lady all dressed up and in her high heels and out of the house. Mike Carroll would accompany us. He said Gottlieb "was the sweetest man." Mort used to talk to her about the theater and you'd just see her sparkle. He'd tell her what their competitors were doing. And when they'd part, she would be rejuvenated because she had had a little stimulation.

Mike would find out about it and he would come home and go into one of his tirades, and, honest to God, she would be better. Mike was ready to kill Gottlieb, and right down the street, at the Lido Apartments, was Phyllis McGuire.

CHAPTER THIRTY-FOUR

MAY STRIKES BACK

Perhaps it was May's marriage to Ed Stanton that gave her the courage to strike out at Helen one last time. Two happenings apparently contributed to her rebellion.

May was very proud of the blooded Suffolk sheep and Black Angus cattle she raised on her farm on the vast grounds surrounding her Petite Trianon. She became angry because she felt *The Post* hadn't given the proper attention to prizes her livestock won in its news coverage of an important show.

Compounding this slight were the stories about her sister she saw in *The Post*, about her plays, her acting roles, her fifty-thousand-dollar annual gifts to the Community Chest, and so on, ad nauseum. She called Palmer Hoyt and told him she was sure Helen had ordered that her name not appear in the newspaper and said she was indignant at him for carrying out her sister's orders. She wound up the conversation by threatening to do something drastic—sell her stock.

Then, when Clyde Berryman died on July 30, 1959, at the age of seventy-eight, she was furious about the obituary that appeared in *The Post* the next day. She called Hoyt and stormed, "You're airing all that dirty linen again."

Papa's Girl

Actually, only two of the obituary's seven paragraphs had anything to do with her marriage to Clyde Berryman. One said: "He was the former husband of May Bonfils, daughter of the late Frederck G. Bonfils, co-founder of *The Denver Post*." The other read, "He was born May 8, 1881, in Central City, Nebraska. He was married to Miss Bonfils November 7, 1904, in Golden. The couple was divorced in 1947."

The story wasn't prominently displayed. It was the next to last of five obituaries published on page forty-six that day. It was the mention of the divorce that really raised her hackles, of course.

May complained to Hoyt that the publicity was unwanted and it was undoubtedly Helen's doing (as it may have been, but the mention of her divorce was legitimate news). "You have maligned me," she told him. "This is the last straw. You are going to regret this story."

With that, May decided to make good on her threat. May's stock—like Helen's—had been wonderfully lucrative. In the fourteen years between 1935 and 1948, *The Post* had paid $19,800,000 in dividends. May's fifteen per cent share brought her almost $3 million dollars, or an average annual income of more than $200,000, a huge amount in those years. Although she spent lavishly, she also invested shrewdly in blue-chip stock, land, antiques, works of art, and jewels.

But after Palmer Hoyt's arrival, *The Post*'s antiquated equipment was replaced, its staff expanded and reporters were sent throughout the country and around the world to cover stories. Dividends were slashed in 1949 to pay for a new plant and never returned to the golden era May so fondly recalled.

In the ten years between 1949 and 1958, *The Post*'s dividend payments totaled $5,534,000. May's share was $830,000—or less than a third of what she had become accustomed to receiving in palmier times. Being almost totally ignorant about the workings of the newspaper, she decided that *The Post* was being mismanaged by Helen and the publisher she had employed to run it. She even expressed the suspicion that Helen was charging a large part of her living expenses to the paper.

May had always dismissed any thought of selling her stock; she was afraid Helen might get hold of it and increase her control. But now, she made contact with Allen Kander, a "finder" of newspapers and television and radio stations for sale. Among his clients was Samuel Newhouse, who had approached Helen in 1959 in New York about buying *The Post*.

At the time, Mr. Newhouse had told Helen, "I would pay you at least twenty million for the paper, and if you will show me some figures, I might be willing to pay considerably more." Of course, he was talking about one hundred per cent of the stock, which Helen didn't have. And, of course, Helen found his offer unwelcome.

So when Mr. Kander went to Newhouse in the spring of 1960 about buying May's minority interest in *The Post*, Newhouse jumped at the chance. In 1960, May sold her stock to Newhouse for $260 a share, or around $4.5 million dollars. She held on to ten shares and stipulated that in the event of her death, her husband was not to sell them as long as Helen was alive.

Helen learned that one provision of the contract was that when Newhouse gained a majority of the stock, May would be named honorary chairman of the board. "Of all the unmitigated gall!" Helen stormed. And May's spite spewed forth in an interview she gave at this time to Gene Cervi, editor of *Cervi's Journal*, a Denver business weekly.

Gene was a friend of May's attorney, Edgar McComb, which probably explains how the *Journal* got the story. Gene had been a reporter at *The Post*, and what May didn't realize was that he was a friend of Helen's as well.

"I was Papa's girl, not Helen," May told Cervi heatedly. "Papa took me on the trips, hunting in Africa. He didn't take Helen. He intended that I should be as important at the paper as Helen.

"She had no right to build that theater for herself so she could show off her acting," she protested.

When Cervi asked if May had been invited to the opening of *The Post*'s new building in 1950, he wrote that "she cried in her high, squeaky voice, 'No. I don't want anything from those burglars down there but my money.'"

The publisher described May as "solidly built, amply bosomed and shorter than her sister, Helen, naturally older, slow-walking and somewhat handsome of face if only she would have that wart removed from the side of her nose." May was then seventy-seven.

May told Cervi that more than a few persons had tried to effect a reconciliation of the sisters, adding, "but they don't know what it is all about and they should stop trying to butt in."

Cervi wrote that the Stantons discussed investing in his *Journal* with the idea of using it to try to bring Helen down a notch or two. He confessed himself dumbstruck at the wealthy couple's assumption that he would be so compliant as to go along with their plans.

Later, he said, May called him from time to time with ideas for stories that would show Helen in a bad light. He never followed up on any of these suggestions. Because of the maliciousness of May's attack, Gene didn't write about his meeting with her until after her death in March 1962.

May's bitterness had also spilled over in a news release she issued at the time she reported the sale of her *Post* stock in 1960. The handout was accompanied by a very handsome (and wildly flattering) reproduction of a portrait of May which had been painted the previous year in Florence by an Italian artist.

After explaining that her decision to sell to Newhouse was "based on carefully studied reports from all cities where Mr. Newhouse operates his many newspapers," the report went on:

"As May Bonfils, Mrs. Stanton traveled extensively with her father in Europe, Asia, and Africa, as well as throughout the United States. She was his constant companion during the early years he operated *The Post* and the Sells-Floto Circus." (Actually, May was off in college in 1903 when Mr. Tammen and Papa bought the circus.)

The report continued: "Mrs. Stanton reputedly is one of the wealthiest women in the West and has been the donor of many personal generous gifts. They include the Monastery for the Franciscan Order in Denver, many building improvements at Loretto Heights College, the May Bonfils Free Cultural Series at the college, improvements to the Villa Nazareth Orphanage for Boys in Rome, together with many scholarships and student funds.

"Her most recent gift was a wing at the Denver Museum of Natural History (now the Denver Museum of Nature and Science) named in honor of her father," Cervi wrote.

CHAPTER THIRTY-FIVE

EXIT MAY

May did not live to see what happened after she unlocked a Pandora's box of problems for her sister with the sale of her *Post* stock. She died in March 1962, in the bed in which Marie Antoinette had slept at Versailles, four years before the beginning of the bitter suits that were fought for control of *The Post*.

DOROTHY RADER

At the time of May's death, Helen was appearing as Regina in *The Little Foxes* at the Bonfils Theatre. None of us was allowed to mention her sister's passing to her that night. When Helen was finally told, she said, "There has been nothing between us for a long time." She did not attend the funeral.

FATHER JOHN ANDERSON
Helen's Priest

I really think Helen would have liked a reconciliation with her sister, but May would have nothing to do with her. Helen was the type of person who would have been happy to have a relationship with her sister.

ROBERT WELSH
Family Friend, Executor

May tore up the prenuptial agreement she had with Ed Stanton, because he made so much money for her from the proceeds she received from the stock sale. She left almost half of her estate, including Belmar, to him. Ed showed a philanthropic bent and a sensitivity to his wife's interests by donating the Petite Trianon and its grounds to the Denver Catholic Archdiocese to be used as a headquarters facility. However, a year later, in 1971, the archdiocese said the mansion was too expensive to maintain and had it demolished.

Principal beneficiaries of the remainder of May's estate were the Orders of Friars Minor, Province of the Most Holy Name and Loretto Heights College. A decade after May's death the real estate and other assets in the trust were valued at $30 million.

Ed sold some of the adjoining hundreds of acres at Wadsworth Boulevard and West Alameda Avenue to be developed for the Villa Italia Shopping Center. By 2003, the shopping center had been demolished to make way for a municipal center for the city of Lakewood. Much of the estate where deer once nibbled and blooded cattle lowed has been developed as a park. There was enough land left over for a new shopping mecca, Belmar.

Ed Stanton died April 22, 1987, at the age of seventy-nine.

During her lifetime, May contributed other millions of dollars to build a Catholic chapel at the Air Force Academy; to establish the May Bonfils Clinic of Ophthalmology at the University of Colorado Medical Center; and to rebuild St. Elizabeth's Catholic Church in Denver.

Like Helen, May wanted desperately for Denver to remember the Bonfils name with respect, and to this end she gave with great generosity. Unlike Helen, she had no foundation to draw upon in giving to the community from which she had remained so remote.

CHAPTER THIRTY-SIX
THE BATTLE TO SAVE THE POST

When May sold her fifteen per cent of *Post* stock to Samuel Newhouse, she let the evil genie out of the bottle as far as Helen was concerned. In June 1966, in an effort to block Newhouse from obtaining additional *Denver Post* stock, Helen paid the Denver United States National Bank more than $5 million of her own money for shares which the bank held in trust for the Children's Hospital and Helen Crabbs Rippey, a niece of Agnes Tammen's. May and Helen were the only direct descendants of the co-founders of *The Post*. Mrs. Tammen had left the bulk of her estate to Children's Hospital and to Helen Rippey.

On July 16, 1966, a suit was filed against the bank, *The Post*, and Helen in U.S. District Court in the names of two of Helen Rippey's sons, Bruce and Gordon.

In October, Judge William E. Doyle ruled that the bank did indeed breach its trust obligation when it sold the stock to Helen for three hundred dollars a share. However, he found no conspiracy between *The Post* management and the bank, so the complaints against *The Post* and Helen were dismissed. But he pegged the value of the stock at $450 a share and imposed a surcharge of $150 per share, which Helen had to pay.

Papa's Girl

It was a very costly victory. The stock couldn't be taken from Helen or the Helen G. Bonfils' Foundation, but she would have to pay an additional $2,600,000, and change. Including legal fees, the deal had cost her more than $8 million.

"Woody, I feel like I'm naked," she told her friend Father Woodrich, the Catholic chaplain at St. Joseph's Hospital, after the payment.

CHAPTER THIRTY-SEVEN
DONALD SEAWELL'S ASCENDANCY

After *The Post* was saved, there was still the question: What would become of it?

At the beginning of 1961, Helen was seventy-one years old, her health was not robust and thoughts of mortality were beginning to intrude.

Since the 1950s, Palmer had talked to Helen about leaving the newspaper in the hands of the employees. All of *The Post* stock except what she owned was tied up in various trusts and foundations which were more concerned about the newspaper's profits than its excellence.

Palmer didn't believe this was a healthy situation. He also thought that the men and women who worked for the paper—the clerks, typesetters, ad salesmen, and reporters as well as executives—should have the opportunity to invest in its ownership and earn the right to share the profit of their labors.

The idea appealed to Helen. And it grew even more appealing when she learned from the paper's executives that Mike was talking about what he would do when he owned *The Post*; in fact, he was boasting in Las Vegas that he already owned the paper.

Helen had not spent $8 million only to have Papa's paper fall into Mike's hands. No, *The Post* must continue under strong, professional leadership.

Palmer said, "Helen, if you want to provide for employee ownership after your death, it would be even more gratifying to start the plan now while you can enjoy the act of giving."

On February 24, 1961, Helen agreed to help get an employees' ownership plan underway with a gift of 1600 shares of her personally held stock. At a price of $260 per share, the gift was worth $416,000. The delight and appreciation of the employees more than justified her action. They had been afraid the paper would end up in the hands of Catholic Charities and other philanthropies.

Then, with Donald Seawell's guidance, Helen rewrote her will to provide that, if she died first, the half of her estate Mike Davis would be entitled to under Colorado law would come from assets other than *The Denver Post* stock. To make doubly sure Mike would not get the paper, she gave all her Post stock to the Helen G. Bonfils Foundation, which could dispose of it only to the Employees Stock Trust. Safeguarding *The Post* had turned her into a mother lion protecting her cub.

Throughout the battle to save *The Post*, Seawell had made himself ever more indispensable. As early as 1959, Helen had told editor Palmer Hoyt that she wanted him to consult with Don on any major decison affecting the paper. Palmer had raised an eyebrow at this request. Nevertheless, Palmer called Donald in New York daily, and Seawell began attending directors' meetings in Denver when business of any importance was to be considered.

DONALD SEAWELL
Helen's Attorney

By the 1960s Helen's health was deteriorating rather badly and she was spending more and more time in the hospital. She said I just had to take care of her as far as *The Post* was concerned.

In 1960, when E. Ray Campbell retired as president of *The Post*, Helen asked me to take the position. I protested that it would be unseemly for a virtual stranger to take over as head man at *The Post*. If Helen would take the title of president, I told her, I would spend half my time in Denver as secretary-treasurer of the corporation with the understanding that I would be acting for her as chief executive officer. I did not want at that time to give up my New York and London law practices.

She also asked me to take over with respect to the theatrical interests and the foundation. Our relations were very close in the theater and at *The Post*. I enjoyed her company very much. Naturally, it was flattering when she said to me, "I'm turning over complete control of *The Post* and foundations to you, because I think you will do the right thing."

One thing that is not generally understood about Helen is that she was a very persuasive and powerful lady. Most people tend to think of her as a very sweet, warm, tender individual—which she was—but no one ever took undue influence of Helen; she's the one who influenced the ones she came in contact with.

Helen admired certain individuals; Jack Kennedy was one of them. I remember Helen saying to me, "I just hope Palmer will support Jack Kennedy."

I said, "Helen, it's your newspaper; you run things. Tell him who he should support."

"Oh, I couldn't do that," she said.

I said, "I'm going to call Ep up to the office right away." I called and he came lumbering up from his second floor office to my suite on the third. After the usual lovey-dovey stuff, Helen finally said, "Ep, Don thinks you ought to know that I'd like for the paper to support Kennedy."

Ep said, "Of course, it's a great idea."

Whether or not he would have done this if I hadn't spoken, I don't know. He had supported Republicans for president until then. In addition to being a great editor, Ep was diplomatic enough to cater to Helen and her known desires.

WILLIAM HOSOKAWA
Palmer Hoyt Biographer

Palmer Hoyt had decided, after an hour-long meeting with Jack Kennedy, that Kennedy was a very astute young man. He assigned two members of the editorial page staff to prepare position papers, one on the side of endorsing Kennedy, the other on Nixon. Only after he had studied these reports did Hoyt finally decide to back Kennedy. That night Hoyt told his wife, Helen May, of his decision. She was a staunch Nixon supporter. The news upset her so much that she said she would telephone Henry Cabot Lodge, Nixon's running mate and another old Hoyt friend, to see if he couldn't change her husband's mind.

 The next morning, Hoyt was meeting with twelve or fifteen men in his office. It became apparent that most of the editors favored Kennedy. He was halfway through a poll of them when his secretary opened the door and told him there was an important long-distance telephone call. Hoyt excused himself. Through the half open door, his rumbling voice could be heard clearly. "Yes, Cabot," they heard him say. "Now Cabot, if you were going to be the candidate there would be no question of our stand, but we just can't go for Nixon. Our editors are unanimous for Kennedy. I'm afraid that's the way it's going to be."

CHAPTER THIRTY-EIGHT

THE ILLUSTRIOUS EX-TIGERS

JO WRIGHT
Secretary to Mike Davis

Mike's former employees have an alumni group. We call ourselves The Outstanding, Illustrious Legion of Ex-Tigers, or TOILET for short. We meet when the spirit moves us, for drinks and lunch or dinner. Then we reminisce and laugh about that time in our lives that seems incredible to us now.

I had been secretary to District Attorney Bert Keating. After he died in July 1967, I applied for a job with the Tiger Oil Company because I heard Mike Davis paid the highest wages in the industry. He surrounded himself with good people and he treated them very well. I worked for him thirteen years, in Denver and in Houston, starting in the late sixties.

I suppose Mike would be called a male chauvinist today. He had a fetish about shoes and wanted female employees to wear high heels. He didn't want wedgies in the office. He didn't like pantsuits. I tried to explain to him that you couldn't make rules about attire in these days of women's rights.

"Well, okay," he'd say sweetly. "They just won't get a raise then."

He'd say, "If you're not happy in your home, you can't work for me." If a divorced woman didn't have custody of her children, he'd say, "Get rid of her."

One Tiger Oil pilot told his wife he would be out of town for several days longer than the actual trip. When the man's wife called the office to check on his return, I took the call. I was trying to cover for him, but, unfortunately, Mike happened to be at my desk.

"What's that?" he said, and took the phone from me. After listening, he said, "Your husband's back in town; he's been here since yesterday. Don't call again." He hung up and he fired the pilot.

Of course, he had a different standard for himself. He'd say, "I'm the one who pays the bills around here."

I've heard he used to wear pinstriped, gangster-like suits, but he'd given those up when I knew him. He had a tremendous wardrobe of 150 beige suits and 100 navy blue suits, all custom made. He was very fastidious.

One time the wife of an oil executive asked him, "Mike, why don't you ever change your clothes?" She didn't realize he had 149 other beige suits and turtlenecks just like the one he was wearing.

He loved cowboy boots, but he never went shopping for them. The salesmen would bring up a rack of boots for his selection and he would choose real alligator at $1,000 a pair. He preferred to see his geologists in wing-tip shoes. He poked fun at the "foo foo" shoes (Hush Puppies) one of his pilots wore.

He could really turn on the charm—especially with the ladies. He swore a lot because that's the way he got his point across. But he never allowed other people in the office to do four-letter words. He'd say, "I use them because I'm the boss and I pay the bills." If anyone let one slip in front of me, they had to apologize.

Sometimes after he'd been swearing a blue streak, he'd say to me, "You know I'm not directing this toward you, and I don't mean to offend." After a while you didn't notice. I've had people apologize to me for his language, and I'd say, "What language?"

He always had a soft spot in his heart for truck drivers because he'd been one. He loved trucks. He had sixty huge oil trucks, Peterbilts.

When the Little Sisters of the Poor called on their rounds of downtown offices, Mike would pull out a roll of bills and start peeling off hundreds. "Is that enough?" he'd say. "Do you want more?" When children would come to his office in the First National Bank Building selling boxes of candy to earn their way to summer camp, he'd say, "I'll buy the whole carton." He'd give them a hundred dollars and their eyes would really light up.

Arthur, who had been George Somnes' butler, was in a nursing home in Switzerland, and when his wife called about their financial difficulties, Mike sent money.

The social side of the oil industry never interested Mike. He seldom drank. At parties, he was known to pour his drink into a planter and order another one.

I don't think he had a social plane. He didn't authorize his people to go to lunch or dinner or conventions on oil business. With the majors, that's their main thing. While I worked for him, I never heard of a coffee break.

There were exceptions. In 1965, he had the "honor" of hosting the annual dance and midnight breakfast for 2,000 delegates to the Denver convention of the American Association of Petroleum Landmen. Each year, this award went to an oilman who was willing and able to pick up the tab. H.L. Hunt, the Texas billionaire, had won the recognition the year before.

At the 1965 event in the downtown Hilton Hotel, Phyllis McGuire sat on the dais with Mike, and Helen Bonfils sat at a table down below with Therese and Paul Messenger, of the (Marvin) Davis Oil Company. "Helen was so proud of him," Mrs. Messenger remembered.

At TOILET get-togethers, we remember the really good times we went through with "the Tige", our boss. One time, Phyllis flew everyone to Las Vegas—first class in a 747—for a surprise party for Mike at the Sands Hotel. The Mills brothers were there, and Louis Prima.

Phyllis was appearing at Harrod's in Reno and at Caesar's Palace in Las Vegas in those days. We treated Phyllis as an equal, not a star. She'd come to our houses.

Another time Mike took everyone to Hawaii. He announced to us one Friday morning that we were going and told everyone, "Call your husband" or "Call your wife. Invite them to come along," he said.

Everyone was saying, "We've got to pack!"

"No, don't take any clothes; we'll get things there," Mike said. A few hours later we took off in his Learjet and the next day we did our shopping for beachwear in Hawaii.

In New York, he'd put his staff up at the River House. Nora and Fanny would fuss over him, and fix him supper at midnight if he came in late.

BILL DURR
Tiger Oil Geologist

I worked for Mike Davis for fourteen years—day and night. He was the last of the great wildcatters. I used to work for Continental Oil Company and I'd work up projects. In a big company you may never know the outcome; Mike gave me that opportunity.

If he heard of something, he'd be on the ground immediately. He didn't care if it was midnight or Christmas Eve. If the play was worth going after, he could move so fast. When someone else would just be talking about it, he would already have done it. He only had a—what?—sixth or eighth grade education, but he was brilliant. He could talk to a petroleum engineer or a geophysicist and it was like he wrote the book.

I don't know of any well drilled by Tiger Oil he didn't go out on. He was on the ground; he called the shots. I think he had a photographic memory. Three years after a well was drilled he could remember the total depth, the zones, why it went dry, and so on.

There were three major oil discoveries in the Rocky Mountain area in the decades between the sixties and eighties, and Mike made two of them happen. They were the Bell Creek area of the Powder River Basin in southwestern Montana and the Red Wing Creek field of the Williston Basin in North Dakota. In a period of ten years, Mike found twenty-three oil fields. He found more oil fields with three geologists than Amoco did with an army of experts.

Being a geologist with Mike Davis meant you got to be introduced to Colonel Moammar Khadafi, the Libyan strongman, and Yasser Arafat, chairman of the PLO, and Adnan Khashoggi, the international arms dealer, in hotel lobbies in the Middle East. Mike would never settle for talking to anyone less than the top guy.

And, in Las Vegas, you'd go backstage to see Johnny Carson after his show, or meet Frank Sinatra, Sammy Davis Jr., Danny Thomas, and Jackie Leonard.

You'd be in an environment—flying to various cities, staying in fine hotels—where it might be tempting to get in a little trouble. But you didn't, because you knew what the consequences would be.

He was strong on family. He loved his mother, and she was a helluva cook. She was always sending us Lebanese bread and cookies. It didn't surprise me when he'd drop a five-hundred-dollar bill in the collection plate in a Catholic church in a small western town when we attended Mass. To him, money was just something that causes things to happen.

R.A. MATUSZCZAK
Tiger Oil Geologist

I give oilman Sam Gary credit for discovering the Bell Creek area. Williston Basin, like many oil discoveries, involved more than one company or individual. Davis wasn't that great an expert, but he worked constantly and he was a real wildcatter, someone who would go out into a remote area, who would try anything at any hour.

HAL JOHNSON
Tiger Oil Land Manager

I wasn't that enthusiastic about Mike's wanting to jump on every new lead, to be on the scene within hours after every discovery, even when it meant rolling out his private jet in the middle of the night. When it came to a play, he had to be on it that minute. Of course, it could have waited a week. I got sick of it the last two years; I had young kids and I wanted to be home.

Once, when I was new to the job, Mike announced he would fly a group of us to a western oil site and then on to Las Vegas. We would leave at once.

The geologists said, "I'll have to pack" and "I have to call my wife."

"Hell, no," Mike said nonchalantly. "We'll be back tonight."

We didn't return to Denver for three weeks. In Las Vegas he paid for changes of clothes for all of us and put us up at the Frontier Hotel. Later on, when he was more flush, we'd stay at the Sands. Mike stayed at Phyllis McGuire's. Every morning we'd show up in the foyer of the house to be "pumped up," to get our daily stipend of a $100 apiece.

Mike never put in an appearance until eleven o'clock, though he'd probably been doing business on the phone since nine. But as it got to be late morning, we'd hear stirrings in another part of the house and male and female voices that carried.

"Why you %#&##!" we'd hear Phyllis. She had a mouth that could match Mike's.

"Izzatso, %#&#!" Mike would come back.

And pretty soon Mike would come striding down the hall in his shorts with a handful of $100 bills.

There was a time when Mike was probably worth from $600 million to $800 million, including reserves, cash, rigs and other equipment.

And I remember a time when his fortunes were real low; he probably had $5,000 in his pocket and that wasn't much for him. We were at a party in Los Angeles, and Mike was giving a hundred bucks to each of the gray-haired members of a combo to play *My Blue Heaven* over and over, and shoving $100 bills down the boobs of the waitresses, and giving bills to the waiters.

BILL DURR
Tiger Oil Geologist

I admire Mike Davis more than anyone I know. He's a sensitive person. He has a heart of gold. He would give you anything he had.

And, wherever he was—the Middle East, Wyoming, Las Vegas—he'd always call Helen.

HAL JOHNSON
Tiger Oil Land Manager

Oh, sure, but he'd call Phyllis first.

R.A. MATUSZCZAK
Tiger Oil Geologist

I heard Mike was offended by the canned music that was piped into the men's room of a large Las Vegas casino he frequented. He complained to the management, and it was arranged for two violinists to be on hand to play whenever he visited the john.

Sometimes, when we were traveling, he would go into a small restaurant in a little town and order everything on the menu. Can you imagine a cook trying to cook everything on the menu? Mike just wanted to see what he liked best.

CHAPTER THIRTY-NINE

A Banquet

MIKE CARROLL
Bodyguard

Mike Davis is a rude, repulsive sonofabitch, but he has a heart as big as this couch and I love him.

On cook's night out we would go out to dinner, Miss Helen, Mike and me. Sometimes we would go to Gaetano's. Mike liked to hang out with gangsters. He thought he was tough, but he couldn't whip a sick whore.

But this night there was just Mike and me at Le Profile, a French restaurant near the chateau, Miss Helen's home. A new waiter showed us to a little table, and Mike exploded, "I don't want to sit here, godammit!"

The maitre d' hurried over and we were seated at a large table. Mike and I ordered dinners and then he ordered six more dinners. People were looking at us like we were crazy when the waiter kept bringing plates of food and putting them on the table before these empty chairs.

After dinner, Mike sent $100 to the cook and $100 to the maitre d'. Then he nods to all the plates of food on the table and says to the waiter, "there's your tip; eat it."

The servants liked Mike in a way. Miss Helen was tight; she'd give them a pair of hose or a scarf at Christmas. Mike would give them $100. But they adored her.

Mike was a great gambler. All he played was roulette. I've seen him drop $60,000, $150,000. He didn't make it too many times. He didn't give a damn about money. All he wanted to do was work.

DR. FRANK MCGLONE
Helen's Physician

Mike got sick with a rectal problem, and he went to the Mayo Clinic. Several doctors there refused to take care of him, but he finally got one. He had X-rays of his diverticulum and he put them up in his plane so everyone could see them.

Before he went to Mayo, Mike Carroll, his bodyguard, insisted on a doctors' conference. There were several doctors present. Mike would never introduce anyone, so no one knew who was who. There was one fellow with a black bag who kept chiming in all the time. Mike Carroll came to the door and called to him, "Hey, Jerry, you're not doing anything. Why don't you come out here and cut my hair?" He was Jerry Middleton, Mike's barber.

CHAPTER FORTY

THE FINAL YEARS

Several times over the years, Helen's physician, Frank McGlone, had said to her, "Helen, this time you really must go to St. Joseph's, or I can't be responsible." And of course, each time she would say no. But at last, she had no choice.

DR. FRANK MCGLONE
Helen's Physician

Helen developed some heart problems and also diabetes in her later years and she just gradually went downhill. Part of the blood clot that had developed in her lung in the '50s caused scar tissue so she didn't have complete lung capacity, and that was a strain on her heart.

In 1967, I had a call from her nurse, Ursula Sievers, that Helen was in a diabetic coma. I checked and found her sugar was 750; normal was 80 to 120. I called an ambulance to take her to St. Joseph's. I thought it best that she stay in the hospital. She had a suite on the eighth floor and I thought she was better protected there from people she didn't want to see. She didn't like Mike; she didn't like Don.

Father John Anderson, Helen's priest and one of her favorite people, was at her bedside when she died.
Courtesy of The Denver Post.

FATHER JOHN ANDERSON
Helen's Priest

One day in 1967, I went over to the house for lunch and Helen wouldn't eat. At 5:00 that afternoon they called me. They had rushed her to St. Joseph's Hospital in a diabetic coma. Except for brief periods she was there until she died in 1972. When she was fourteen she had tuberculosis, and one lung collapsed. She had been diagnosed a diabetic in 1967. She did wonderfully well in spite of it all. She had a great will.

After she entered St. Joseph's, we used to go every day to the Pencol Drug Store on East Colfax for a soda. And if you don't think that created a sensation—a nurse; a chauffeur; Missie, a collie-type dog; me, a priest; and Helen, who was always such a presence. Of course, Helen was so gracious to everyone. "Would you like to see the play at Elitch's?" she'd ask the young people behind the counter.

URSULA SIEVERS
Helen's Private Nurse

Mike insisted there should be two extra nurses, in addition to Miss Merlino and me. It was all just for show. He was there at the hospital practically all the time.

That Christmas, she wanted to give fur coats to Joyce Merlino and me because we had been with her the longest. She told me, "I know just the fur you have to get." It would have to be custom made because I am so big, a size eighteen. She had Jonas Brothers bring up pelts; mine would be Black Diamond, and Joyce's Autumn Haze.

Mike said, 'honey, you cannot buy two nurses fur coats and not make the others feel bad." She argued with him for an hour about it. In the end, she also bought fur coats for the other two nurses.

In the hospital, her entertainment was every Friday. She'd have lunch with Father Anderson and any friend who happened to be in the hospital, like Ellie Weckbaugh and Virginia Buell or Gene Cervi. The table would be set with linens and silver and china and we would have it catered. She always wanted me to join them and treated me just like anyone else.

Her furs and jewels were in a closet. She went out on special occasions, like the opening of her Broadway play, *Sleuth*, at City Auditorium, or a retirement party for her fashion editor, Gretchen Weber, at the University Club.

FATHER CHARLES B. "WOODY" WOODRICH
Pastor, Holy Ghost Church

I became chaplain at St. Joseph's in 1969, during Helen's last years there, and I saw her practically every day. If I missed seeing her, she'd give me hell.

She asked to receive communion every day. The church was really the hidden force in her whole life, her secret blanket. She had a deep love of the church.

She built the Holy Ghost Church at the top of the Depression and took money for it off the top of her inheritance. Her parents' wills were in court for ten to twelve years, and when they were finally settled she built Holy Ghost in honor of her father and mother. She wanted a downtown church where working people could go to worship. Reporters, especially, were going to bars instead of Mass.

If there is one monument the bastards aren't going to take the Bonfils name off, it's Holy Ghost. This epitaph has involved her whole life—the love of the church, the poor, the underdog—and it erases as much evil from the Bonfils name as she could.

Papa's Girl

Because it was her church, her favorite priest, John Anderson, became its pastor. He was there for many of the years she went to Mass before going to her office at *The Post*. Basically, Johnny was the only one she could trust. He wasn't looking for anything; he knew her loneliness. He made a lot of sacrifices; he wouldn't take a vacation. Christmas was the loneliest day of her life.

When she was taken to St. Joseph's in a diabetic coma, Johnny was there beside her when she came out of it.

In the hospital, I remember how pitted she was against the growth of Denver—all the big buildings going up. Looking out the window, she'd tell me, "Woody, I'm going to leave a monument everyone in Denver will enjoy." She had a dream of a performing arts center.

The largest event in her life in those years was the opening night of *Sleuth*, January 4, 1972, at the Denver Auditorium. She was dressed all in white—a long white mink coat and gown—and, oh, she looked stunning! She went by wheelchair to the backstage entrance to visit the star, Anthony Quayle. Then she insisted on leaving the chair to walk into the auditorium. "If I can't walk, I won't go," she had said. [Father John Anderson] and I and one of her nurses accompanied her. She stood and greeted people in the lobby during the intermission and then she wanted to leave; she was tired.

I was almost a pauper. I had nothing. My mother was in a nursing home, and Helen sent to Montaldo's and bought her very expensive dresses, shoes, and hats. She was always after me to buy better clothes.

If she read about a tragedy in the paper, she would say, "Woody, write that name down," and I would see that an envelope would be delivered from *The Post* with a check to that person enclosed.

If Sister Mary Andrew at the hospital needed new beds, a new parking lot, or the rugs in the elevator were dirty, she got whatever she needed, all thanks to Helen.

Helen was a very warm, generous, loving person. I have never met the equal of her, from the standpoint of her power with *The Post* or the power and influence she had in the community because of her money. I call her the greatest woman in the history of Denver, and totally forgotten.

My last days at the hospital were rather awkward because I was appointed editor of the *Denver Catholic Register*. Helen said, "I don't care how small you are, you're still competition." She was thinking of the advertising.

About the last six months she was critical, and the *Rocky Mountain News* was calling me every night.

"Woody," Helen told me, "I'm going to die on *Post* time." That meant after midnight, when the *News* had been put to bed.

I became pastor of Holy Ghost in 1972, the year of her death, because Johnny recommended me when he went to a position with the archdiocese. We'd known each other since we were in seminary together. Holy Ghost is one of the most beautiful churches in the country. People come here from Greeley, Fort Collins, Wyoming, the whole West.

You can see the results of her generosity here. Hundreds of hungry people are fed every week, in a sandwich line. When it's bitter cold and the shelter is overflowing, we take as many as we can into the sanctuary.

CHAPTER FORTY-ONE
DIVORCE

DR. FRANK MCGLONE
Helen's Physician

Three or four years before Helen's divorce from Mike came about, Earl Moore, Palmer Hoyt and I talked about that possibility. Earl Moore, the secretary-treasurer of *The Denver Post*, was co-executor of Helen's estate, along with Donald Seawell.

Helen said she didn't want any part of Mike. Earl had the papers ready half a dozen times, and she would say yes in the morning but by noon she'd change her mind. Mike would get to her, and also she didn't want anything in the newspapers. She thought a divorce would be bad publicity, and beyond all things, she didn't want the *Rocky Mountain News* to have the story.

MIKE CARROLL
Helen's Bodyguard

The guards at St. Joseph's were given a picture of Mike Davis and they had instructions not to let him in.

Mike would rant and yell, "She's my wife, you sonofabitch," but the guard would say, "I don't care who you are, you're not getting in."

Seawell didn't want anyone seeing her, even me for a while. I was not supposed to get in, but I did. Miss Merlino would let me in. I used to smuggle Maggie, a little brown dog, the nicest dog, up in the freight elevator to see Miss Helen.

URSULA SIEVERS
Helen's Private Nurse

They shut out Joe Farrow, Mike Carroll, and Jim Powers, her other security guy, and they were her family. When she didn't have control any more, I saw her spirit go. To have so much power and see it go—I saw her depressed. She thought Don Seawell was getting too big for his britches. Toward the end, she was very rude to him; she wouldn't talk to him on the phone.

I think her one concern was to do what was good for *The Post*.

There were guards on her door; one of her lawyers put them on. They had all her calls screened. I asked for the peephole in the door because the sisters would just walk in and ask for whatever they wanted. Helen bought a house across the street to be used for nurses' quarters.

PAULINE CONNOR
Nurse

I was in Miss Helen's room one day as Donald Seawell was leaving. After he had gone, she said to me, "I never meant for him to have so much power."

DONALD SEAWELL
Helen's Attorney

Helen and I were close until the end. I got away from Denver only with difficulty because of her dependence on me. She asked me to go to Rome to receive the Pope's blessing on the Medal of St.

Genecius, patron saint of actors, and the gift of a holy relic, a fragment of bone, which was to be awarded her. I went to Italy, but before I could arrange an audience with the Pope, I got a call that Helen was bad. I asked Helen Hayes to accept the medal from the Pope and I hurried back to Helen's bedside.

There was never an ultimatum to Helen to divorce Mike. There was no danger he could get his hands on *The Post* because of the new will I had drawn for Helen several years before.

She had two great loves, *The Denver Post*—that was foremost—and the theater, that was second.

Helen's marriage to Mike in a civil ceremony in 1959 was not valid in the eyes of the Catholic Church. In one of those seemingly inexplicable acts of which she was capable, she repeated her vows before the Rev. John McCotter in the Mother of God Catholic Church, her parish church, the year following their wedding.

Why? She was blackmailed into her first marriage and bullied into the second. Mike threatened to go to the *Rocky Mountain News* and tell them she was having an affair with him in order to induce her to marry him. She stayed married because she was afraid of what he might do.

Finally, Helen told me she wanted a divorce. "I don't want to die with that name," she said.

"Well, Helen, do you love him?" I asked.

"How could I love a thing like that?" she responded.

A suit charging cruelty was quickly filed thereafter, in the fall of 1971. A decree of divorce was granted December 21, 1971. A private agreement, sealed by court order, was reached on the division of property. Mike received the mansion and all its contents.

FATHER WOODRICH
Pastor, Holy Ghost Catholic Church

I gave communion to Helen almost every day she was in the hospital. If I didn't stop to visit her, she'd give me hell. She loved Mike Davis until the day she died.

FATHER ANDERSON
Helen's Priest

Helen had no doubts she had done the right thing in putting Don in charge of *The Post*. I was with Helen right to the end, and none of those rumors about Don "taking over" ever happened. They're humorous.

How do you explain Mike? I don't know ...

MIKE CARROLL
Helen's Bodyguard

Mike Davis roared like a wounded bull when he was served the divorce papers. Then he remembered his motto, "Money can buy anything." He hired Melvin Belli, the famous San Francisco lawyer, and a former Colorado governor, Stephen L. R. McNichols, among others, to represent him.

In the divorce settlement, Mike received the home at 707 Washington Street and all its contents. He gave everything to Phyllis McGuire. Three vans pulled up.

Workmen packed the antiques Miss Helen said George Somnes had collected and Belle's and Papa's furniture from the Bonfils mansion. Everything was going to Phyllis's home in Las Vegas. They crated the high-backed chair in the hallway, the chair Miss Helen said Papa always sat in. They stripped the library of its wood paneling and took the bookshelves; they removed the marble fronts of fireplaces, took down the chandeliers, and pulled up the rugs. They pried away the smoked-glass ceiling in the dining room. They took everything, even the lightbulbs.

I had to leave. Christ, I was crying. There was nothing left for me to guard. I asked to be relieved of my duties.

Phyllis sold the mansion to a group of local developers for a condominium-townhouse for $3 million in 1984.

CHAPTER FORTY-TWO

THRENODY II

URSULA SIEVERS
Helen's Private Nurse

June 1972.
Because Dr. McGlone was ill with hepatitis, he asked Dr. George Curfman to attend Miss Helen in her final days.

I went off-duty the evening of June 1. I kissed her when I was leaving, and we said goodbye to each other. I had an uneasy premonition.

I had gotten Dr. Curfman to let me start an IV—an intravenous transfusion—on her, because I didn't think it would look good for the owner of *The Denver Post* to die dehydrated.

Father Anderson took his place beside her.

FATHER ANDERSON
Helen's Priest

The last days were pretty brutal for her. Saturday, she was having a difficult time with her breathing. Sunday, she was sitting up and alert. Monday, she was starting to fail. Tuesday she was pretty conscious until about suppertime. She died about 2:10 Wednesday morning. I was holding on to her hand. She kind of reached out and then just slumped back. In one hand she held the St. Genesis medal the Pope had blessed.

She died, as she had said she would, on *Post* time.

THE POSTER
The Denver Post Employee Newspaper

A memoir bordered in yellow roses, Miss Helen's favorite flower, read:

> Miss Helen once picked out a hat she liked at a small shop near *The Post* building.
>
> The clerk remarked: "Oh, Miss Helen, you'll see the same one on every street corner in Denver."
>
> Miss Helen smiled and answered, "That's perfectly all right, you see *The Denver Post* on every street corner, too."
>
> That's the way she was and that's why we loved her and will never forget ...

HENRY LOWENSTEIN
Set Director, The Bonfils Theater

After Helen's death, when her distant relatives went to court in an attempt to break her will, they tried to claim she was not in her right mind at the end. But she had a helluva good head on her. Two days before she died, we were discussing the upcoming season at the Bonfils.

THE FUNERAL

The Mass of Resurrection was in Holy Ghost Catholic Church, the downtown Denver church Helen had built as a memorial for Belle and Frederick Bonfils at East Nineteenth Avenue and Broadway. Father Anderson assisted Archbishop James V. Casey in celebrating

Mass at the flower-banked altar. Yellow roses covered the coffin. A card read, "From the Employees of *The Denver Post*," but the spray had been ordered by Donald Seawell, who knew them to be her favorite flower.

Archbishop Casey eulogized, "Great as is this church, great as the many other chairities accomplished through her, I suspect the greatest happiness came not so much from the public manifestations of her goodness. Rather, her deepest satisfaction came from the countless, hidden times she never let the world know what her right hand was doing ... when she provided love for the unloved, hope for the depressed, inspiration for those striving for excellence. Her life was truly a love story. She loved people as they were, the great, and equally, the insignificant, children and adults, the uneducated and the wise, the sick and the healthy, the poor and the rich, the saints and the sinners. She loved all without distinction of race or color or creed or culture."

The city's dignitaries, some of whom had cursed her father but had come to admire—even love—his youngest daughter, were seated alongside the luckless friends she had helped over the years. There were business leaders, personages who peopled the *Denver Social Register*, theater folk, *Post* employees and their bosses, and just ordinary Coloradans.

"Mike was seated over to one side, like he wasn't supposed to be there," Ursula Sievers said.

"Joe Farrow and Mike Davis sat together the third row back from the altar," Mike Carroll recalled. "They were the only ones on that side. They barred Mike from going to the cemetery in the funeral cortege, so I rode out with him in the green Lincoln. I said, "Now, Mike, don't cause any trouble."

He said, "I'm not. I just want to be there."

As the coffin was placed in the Bonfils family crypt at Fairmount Cemetery, "I remember Mike leaning on the coffin, crying, crying, crying," Father Woodrich said.

In death, Helen was reunited with her first husband George Somnes, whose coffin was adjacent to hers in the magnificent Bonfils memorial crypt.

Papa's Girl

MIKE CARROLL
Helen's Bodyguard

Miss Helen's coffin was in a vault above her father and mother. In front, completely separate, is May's vault.

Joe Farrow was the only one of the employees who got a pension. I understand Nora and Fanny and Arthur were taken care of. Donald Seawell said to me, "You don't get anything; you've had enough." Miss Helen sent my son Mike to college. He had a car, he didn't even have to buy a pencil. I had a car. Still, I didn't appreciate what he said.

CHAPTER FORTY-THREE

ROBERT STOUFFER
Chauffeur

The last time I saw Helen was in 1959, in the hallway of my apartment building, where she had come to arrange an apartment for a woman friend. She embraced me and was very cordial. She introduced me to a fellow who she said was driving for her. Not long after that I read in the paper that she had married the fellow, Mike Davis, who was less than half her age. I understand she financed Mike when he began wildcatting; that he was very lucky in this and is now worth more than she is.

When I felt able, after my dismissal by Helen and George in 1950, I applied for a job in *The Post* machine shop, intent upon making use of my previously acquired mechanical training in New Jersey. Neither Helen nor any of the *Post* higher-ups at first knew of my employment there.

In spite of the new presses (purchased by Palmer Hoyt), the papers were coming off smeared with ink so that they were barely readable. Rubber ink rollers were torn and bearings were being burned out. I was put on the job of trying to rectify this. On going over the press blueprints, I found that the rollers had not been installed in the proper order, and that they were adjusted so close that when the presses were speeded up, the rollers expanded and thereby caused the trouble.

Major Bonfils (who was a nephew of F.G.'s whom he had put in as business manager) was responsible for the mistakes. He resented my working there—no doubt thinking that I was sent to spy on him. Being in charge of pay rates, he refused to let me have a full machinist's wage.

After getting the presses working properly so that they turned out a legible newspaper, I tendered my resignation. When the pressroom foreman, Harry Bergstrum, heard that I was quitting he became very angry. He said I had done a fine job and that there never had been such agreeable cooperation between the machine shop and the press room. He said that the Major was crazy and that he would call the pressmen out on strike. I told him that I didn't want to cause any trouble over my leaving.

Nick DeGeorge, master mechanic, begged me to reconsider and said he would see that I received top wages. I didn't complain to anyone, but after I left, the Major was asked to resign.

Realizing that it was imperative that I work again, I took and passed a Civil Service examination and became a file clerk at the Air Force Finance Center. While there I received several oustanding performance awards and promotions. I worked there until 1960 and found that I qualified for Social Security.

During the division of F.G.'s stocks and bonds, they came across a block of stocks that had no market value. Helen said, "We decided to put these certificates in your name for we know Papa wanted you to have more than the amount in his will. If they ever become of any value you'll profit by it, and if they remain worthless you will not be out anything."

As I did not have a safety deposit box at the time, Helen offered to put them in her vault, in an envelope marked as her property. Later on when I rented a safety deposit box and asked Helen for the certificates, she said she would get them for me, but she never did. In a few years the stock began to pay dividends which, of course, came to me.

When I left Helen's employ and asked for them, she refused to turn them over, saying, "These belong to me, but you can continue to get the dividends, and if I sell the stock I'll give you half of the proceeds." In answer to a letter I wrote, the company verified that I was the owner of the stock. In 1965, after a hospital confinement, I realized that in case of my death, my daughter, Betty, might have difficulty in getting possession of the certificates. So I engaged an attorney who finally secured them for me in 1967. By that time the stocks' valuation had greatly increased, as had the dividends.

CHAPTER FORTY-THREE

LIFE GOES ON IN LAS VEGAS

SHIRLEY EADER
Syndicated Columnist

In the mid-seventies, I was in Las Vegas and I ran into the entertainers Mary Healey and Peter Lind Hayes. "Before you go home, you have got to go to Phyllis McGuire's for dinner," they said.

An invitation was arranged, and when my husband and I arrived with Mary and Peter, we entered the home through a doorway that was a replica of the Paris Arc de Triomphe.

The house was as big as two football fields. If you went right, you'd walk into a replica of the Eiffel Tower. On the other side was a dining room with a mirrored ceiling that reflected the kitchen so that it appeared the help were walking on the ceiling.

All of a sudden, in comes this guy, short with a big cigar in his mouth, wearing a yellow jumpsuit. He said, "Phyllis is downstairs, getting a massage. She'll be up pretty soon. I'm Mike Davis. I live here; it's my house."

Phyllis came up and she was wonderful. She looked pretty as a picture. She took me into the living room. It had to be one hundred feet long. It looked like a furniture store. The furniture was breathtaking, things I haven't seen outside a museum. But so much of it! There was a great stand with a huge book on it. It was Helen Bonfils' family Bible. Phyllis said, "She left this to Mike." A lot of the furniture and the paneling came from the Helen Bonfils mansion in Denver, she said.

There were dozens of graceful French antique chairs and settees, and blazing chandeliers and elegant lamps, all reflected in ornately framed mirrors. A tapestry-patterned Aubusson rug covered a portion of the gleaming black and white marble floor. The collection of fans that circled the room on a molding below the ceiling had also been Helen's, Phyllis said.

While we were nibbling caviar and sipping champagne, Phyllis said, "we're waiting for someone." Finally, she decided dinner shouldn't be delayed any longer.

We sat down at the dining room table. Three Filipino servants served the seven guests. Phyllis said the extra man at the table was her accompanist. She said they traveled with Johnny Carson and it was Mike's plane that flew them.

After the second course, Mike Davis was called to the telephone. He came back and said, "It was Bunky. He's been busy buying stamps and horses. He'll be here for dessert." He ordered another place set at the table.

Then the doorbell rang and Mike said, "It's gotta be Bunky." He trotted off after the butler to welcome his guest and in comes this little fellow, who is Bunker Hunt, who had just lost millions trying to corner the silver market.

He was wearing an ill-fitting suit with a jacket he couldn't button. It was just terrible looking.

Mike says, "Whaddaya want, Bunky? I know you like prune whip." And out comes Jell-O and cakes and pudding, and Bunky ate them all. Bunky was glad to see Mike and he was very polite and well-mannered. Mike says to Bunky, "I want to show you something," and we went out and saw a lake filled with white swans.

Then we went to a "nightclub" downstairs, which even had a neon sign. The dance floor was in the shape of a piano. Phyllis sang six or seven songs before Bunky said he would have to leave to fly back to Texas.

"How'd ya like the prune whip, Bunky?" Mike asked.

Bunky said it was very good and he was very appreciative of the evening.

Phyllis announced, "Now we're going to hear Mike sing." So Mike sang several songs, and he sounded terrible. My husband, Ed, was falling asleep.

It was the best evening I ever spent.

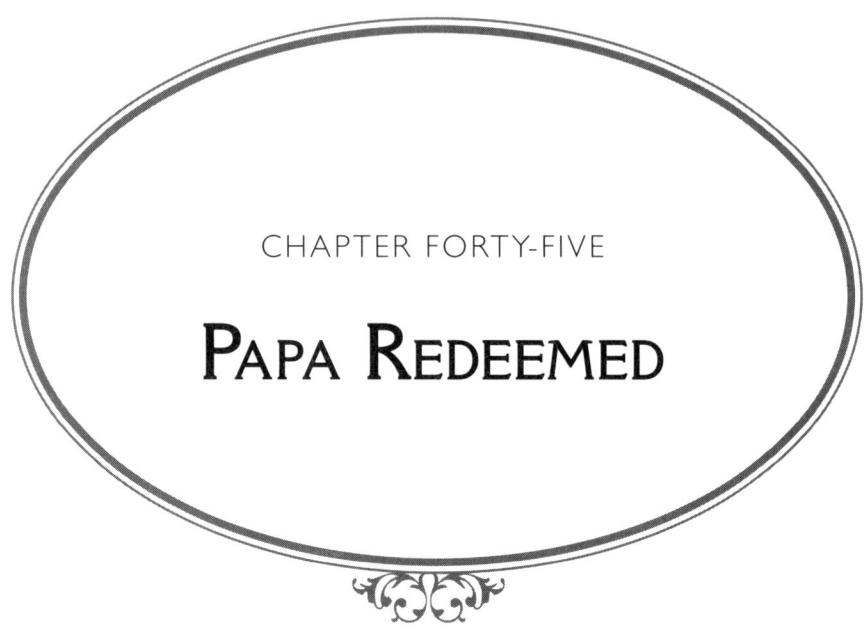

CHAPTER FORTY-FIVE

PAPA REDEEMED

Helen kept a book by her bedside entitled, *Papa's Sayings*.

She often thumbed through it, and was fond of quoting Papa whenever the opportunity arose—which, of course, was quite often.

One of Bonfils' sentiments was, "It's better to be criticized for saving money than being a hobo."

Another: "It is immoral to throw away money in large tips to waiters. It only spoils a man to overpay him. Never do it. It means you're afraid of something—of appearing ridiculous, perhaps—when you give a big tip."

Helen must have thought Papa would twirl in his grave like a Turkish dervish if he had lived to see the liberal tips Mike tossed out so casually. He thought nothing of giving a $100 bill to a gape-jawed parking attendant. Waiters, waitresses and maitre'ds were treated with similar largesse. When friends expressed amazement, Mike would shrug and say, "What the hell; they don't get no respect or satisfaction out of life."

F.G. Bonfils was made from a very different cut of cloth, of course. But, as Helen knew, he was not always the miserly penny-pincher he was often made out to be.

For instance, Helen was proud of the twenty acres between Eighth and Eleventh Avenues on Colorado Boulevard that Papa gave as a site for the University of Colorado Medical School in 1922 "as an unrestricted gift to the people of Colorado."

Papa was very interested in medical research. Through the Frederick G. Bonfils Foundation, he offered prizes for the cure of tuberculosis, a scourge in his day, and for the conquest of cancer. The Foundation's millions were also (rather vaguely) intended to be used "for the betterment of mankind ... for better schools, better and more intelligent people and healthier and happier conditions of life."

In the end, it wasn't medical research, but entertainment—one of Bonfils' great loves, and, really, the essence of his news empire—that benefited so munificently from the millions in the Helen Bonfils (formerly the Frederick G. Bonfils) Foundation.

On one mild day after Helen Bonfils' estate was settled, Donald Seawell sat on a curb in a run-down section of downtown and sketched his vision of a performing arts center.

Helen had envisioned a theater, something all the people of Denver could enjoy, she said, but nothing on the scale her attorney was so intently drawing.

DONALD SEAWELL
Helen's Attorney

The idea of a performing arts center wasn't entirely altruistic, because at an earlier time when we were thinking of enlarging the Bonfils (theater) we were still fighting to get permanent control of *The Post*.

Then along comes the Tax Reform Act of 1969, which says that no foundation could maintain control over a corporation. That meant that over a period time the Bonfils Foundation would have to sell off control of *The Post*—exactly what we had been fighting to avoid.

There was a provision of the Tax Reform Act that Arthur Goldberg (former U.S. Supreme Court Justice and *Denver Post* counsel) and I had testified in favor of. It excepted foundations that were satellites of public foundations, and in this case the public foundation was the Denver Center for the Performing Arts. That also meant we could continue to feed *Denver Post* stock into the Employees Stock Trust.

The question really was whether a foundation of this size could do more by concentrating on one need of the community or by trying to be Santa Claus to everyone and not succeeding in anything outstanding.

To realize this dream, Seawell leveled a block of run-down small businesses on Fourteenth Street. From their rubble arose a modern, gleaming center with a soaring glass canopy covering three theaters and the Frank H. Ricketson Cinema. (The cinema was eventually converted into a theater also.) Adjoining the Helen G. Bonfils Theatre Complex is the Boettcher Concert Center, a $13 million concert hall, built with funds raised by the Denver Symphony Association and a voter-approved bond issue.

In time, a 2,000-seat theater was built adjoining the concert hall. On the corner at Fourteenth and Lawrence Street, anchoring the cultural edifices, is the venerable Denver Civic Auditorium. In 2002, voters agreed to upgrade the landmark to its turn-of-the-century elegance with a bond issue. The result is the stunning Ellie Caulkins Opera House.

When the Helen Bonfils Theatre Complex was dedicated in December 1979, the Foundation had contributed more than $36 million to its completion. The sizable endowment made the Denver Center "the envy of every arts center in the country," said Geraldine Otremba, deputy operations director for the Kennedy Center in Washington, D.C.

The Denver Center was also a catalyst for the rebirth of Denver's lower downtown, attracting thousands to the once depressed area for a myriad of arts and cultural events.

Papa's Girl

This oil portrait of Helen hangs in the lobby of the Helen Bonfils Theatre Complex at the Denver Center.

HELEN AS PARADOX

As Donald Seawell observed, "Helen was a different person to everyone she met."

There was the Helen who could be quite giddy and girlish about men, and the one who was extremely level-headed about people.

Proud and yet shy, she guarded her privacy closely. Yet, she astonished even her closest friends by marrying her much younger chauffeur, an act guaranteed to put headlines on the front page of the crosstown rival *Rocky Mountain News*.

She performed countless acts of kindness and relief, large and small. Her major gifts to institutions added up to millions. In fact, her compassion for the luckless (not to mention dogs and cats) seemed boundless.

How, then, to account for the callous indifference she heaped upon longtime family retainer Robert Stouffer, whom she had once considered a confidante and friend, when he most needed help?

In this regard, Frederick and Belle Bonfils did not set an admirable example for their two daughters, but perhaps the Bonfils were not so different from other upperclass families of their day in their lack of sensitivity toward their servants. Helen grew up in a different time.

But along with all the paradoxes she presented, there were truths about Miss Helen on which all could agree: She loved *The Denver Post*, she loved the theater, and she worshipped the memory of her father, Frederick Gilmer Bonfils. She was, indeed, "Papa's Girl."

The End

Afterword

2007

Now many, perhaps most, of the players have left the stage.

One exception, at this writing, is Donald Seawell, who celebrated his ninety-fourth birthday in August 2006. He retired in 2006 as chief executive officer and chairman of the board of the Denver Center (formerly the Denver Center for the Performing Arts), but remains chairman emeritus. In the summer of 2007, he still visited his office daily.

In 1998, Seawell had the supreme satisfaction of seeing the Denver Center Theatre Company honored with a Tony, as the "best regional theater" in the country, at Broadway's Antoinette Perry awards in New York.

Helen's name appears on the marquee of the Helen Bonfils Theatre Complex building, the umbrella for four theaters; and the Donald Seawell Ballroom, where many of the city's most festive and imposing events occur. Helen Bonfils' oil portrait, which Seawell commissioned, hangs in the lobby of the theater complex.

Helen's beloved Bonfils Theatre at Elizabeth Street and East Colfax Avenue eventually was renamed the Henry Lowenstein Theatre, then it closed and was shuttered for decades. It was revived briefly for television production in the 1980s; several *Perry Mason* episodes were filmed there. It closed again for several years, then was remodeled and opened as the Tattered Cover bookstore—a new version of a Denver landmark—in 2006.

Tiger Mike Davis, who chose not to be interviewed for this book, lives in Las Vegas where he is on friendly terms with Phyllis McGuire. He still makes an occasional headline with an oil strike.

Postscript

EVA HODGES WATT

After I retired from *The Denver Post* in October 1985, I decided I would like to write a biography of Helen Bonfils, the late chairman of the board of *The Post,* whom I had come to admire over my more than forty-year career with the newspaper. I envisioned my project as a paean of praise for her remarkable generosity to Denver.

My acquaintance with Miss Helen came about because I was one of the few "girl" reporters in a newsroom filled with men, and sometimes a feature story in which she was interested required a "woman's touch." After a story or two, she felt she knew me, and she always preferred to deal with people she knew. In 1950, she requested that I be the reporter assigned to interview her when her editors insisted that she should share her reflections on the move of *The Post* from its storied home on Champa Street to the site of the former City Market on California Street.

Somewhat later, on our last such encounter, I told her I would be leaving *The Post* because I was pregnant. Miss Helen was not one to coo over such news. "I wish you good luck, dear," she said, adding dismissively, "I was never maternal."

My research for this book took me on a journey I had never envisioned. One of my first interviews was with Dr. Osgood Philpott, Miss Helen's dermatologist and friend for some fifty years. I remember that patrician gentleman placing his fingertips together and telling me, in precise terms, of one of Helen's first forays into dating, with "Papa" watching her departure through a window.

I am indebted to Sammy Sugarman, onetime University of Denver football player and owner of Shugie's, a popular bar on East Colfax Avenue, for answering a question that perplexed many Denverites: "Where did Mike Davis come from?"

I took a train from New York to Connecticut to visit Haila Stoddard. She gave me a delectable lunch of *salade Nicoise* and cold ham, and talked for several hours about her good friend and former partner in theatrical ventures. It was growing dark when her husband, Whitfield Connor, returned from his afternoon appointment at the Sloane-Kettering Cancer Center in New York where he was undergoing treatment. He didn't feel like talking at the time. But, later, the three of us got together at Denver's Rattlesnake Club, and Whit contributed his own warm and amusing anecdotes.

Donald Seawell, Helen's attorney and *Post* executive, was generous with his time and eloquent in relating stories of their relationship. Equally helpful were Henry Lowenstein, director of the Bonfils Theatre; Dr. Frank McGlone, her personal physician for many years; her bodyguard Mike Carroll; and other members of Miss Helen's household. They all said they loved her and they were eager to talk about her. I sensed they were pouring out memories pent up during the more than a dozen years since her death.

Then, there was Tiger Mike Davis' merry band of Tiger Oil employees who spoke so nostalgically of the flush times they shared. They, too, admired Helen.

There were a few dissenting voices, of course. Helen May Hoyt complained that Helen "didn't like women; she didn't like wives." And Mimi Hatton, wife of the manager of the Bonfils Theatre, said disapprovingly that "she was man crazy."

Other people I talked to helped flesh out a portrait of Helen Bonfils who, I came to realize, few might recognize. She *was* generous, even more so than I expected. She was, also, a more multifaceted, flesh-and-blood person than I ever dreamed.

A couplet by Robert Browning could sum up her life:

How sad and bad and mad it was—
But then how it was sweet!"

ACKNOWLEDGEMENTS

For help in creating *Papa's Girl*, I am greatly indebted to my daughter-in-law, Laura Watt, and her husband, Joe, for their technological expertise and wise suggestions. My thanks also to my old friend, William Hosokawa, whose book about *The Denver Post*, *Thunder in the Rockies*, was an invaluable source for me; and to the ever-helpful Dr. Tom Noel. I am grateful to *The Denver Post* for its generous contribution of photographs, and, also, to the Western History Department of the Denver Public Library. Finally, for their appreciation of my work, I thank David and Jan Smith and Marty Priest of Western Reflections Publishing Company, and my perceptive editor, Jean Campion.

Eva Hodges Watt

Papa's Girl Sources

INDIVIDUALS:

Leonard Alterman, furniture store owner
The Rev. John Anderson
Helen Marie Black, founder, Denver Symphony Orchestra
Georgia Barber, *Denver Post* society editor
William J. Barker, *Denver Post* columnist
Lydia Barker
Charles Buxton, business manager, *Denver Post*
Mike Carroll, bodyguard
Shelia Bisenius, godchild
Spring Byington, actress
Temple Buell, architect
Whitfield Connor, actor; manager, Elitch's Theatre
Dave Davis, brother of Mike Davis
Bill Durr, Tiger Oil Company geologist
Shirley Eader, columnist
John Eby, public relations, Elitch's Theatre
Joe Farrow, chauffeur
Atwill Gilman
Morton Gotlieb, New York theatrical partner
Harry Lou Gurtler, *Denver Post* society editor
Bradford Hatton
Mimi Hatton
Isabel Holmes, Open Forum editor, *Denver Post*
Helen May Hoyt
Elinor Jenkins, Broadway costume designer
Hal Johnson, Tiger Oil Company landman
Bernadine Kirchof
Christopher Kirkland

Papa's Girl

Jess Kortz, Denver jeweler
Edwin Levy, director, Bonfils Theatre
Henry Lowenstein, director, Bonfils Theatre
David Mathias, Denver Post photographer
R.A. Matuszczak, Tiger Oil Company geologist
Betty Ondrusek-Meyer
Frank McGlone, Helen Bonfils' physician
Mary McGlone
Alexis McKinney, managing editor, *Denver Post*
Teresa Messinger
Jerry Middleton, Mike Davis' barber
Dr. James Monsour
June Monsour
Mary Kay O'Connor
Dr. Osgood Philpott, dermatologist
Dorothy Rader, boxoffice manager, Bonfils Theatre
Frank Ricketson Jr.
Donald Roybal
Donald Seawell, attorney, *Denver Post* executive
Ursula Sievers, nurse
Pat Smedley, *Denver Post* society editor
Haila Stoddard, actress, theatrical partner
Robert Stouffer, Bonfils chauffeur
Tom Stouffer
Sammy Sugarman, owner of Shugie's Lounge
Gretchen Weber, *Denver Post* artist
The Rev. Charles B. (Woody) Woodrich
Jo Wright, secretary to Mike Davis

PUBLICATIONS:

Cervi's Business Journal
The Denver Post
Rocky Mountain News
Westword

Papa's Girl

Saturday Evening Post, "Papa's Girl," by Mary Ellen and Mark Murphy, December 23, 1944

Vanity Fair Magazine, "The Biggest Jewels in Las Vegas. The Private Life of Phyllis McGuire" by Dominick Dunne, June 1989

Thunder in the Rockies, by William Hosohawa. William Morrow & Company

Elitch's Gardens, Denver, Co., A History of the Oldest Summer Theater in the U.S. (1890-1941) Edwin Lewis Levy. A dissertation for Columbia University, Western History Department. Denver Public Library

Robert Stouffer, Memoir

OTHER:

Colorado Historical Society
Western History Department, Denver Public Library